DIS/CORD

Before you start to read this book, take this moment to think about making a donation to punctum books, an independent non-profit press,

@ https://punctumbooks.com/support/

If you're reading the e-book, you can click on the image below to go directly to our donations site. Any amount, no matter the size, is appreciated and will help us to keep our ship of fools afloat. Contributions from dedicated readers will also help us to keep our commons open and to cultivate new work that can't find a welcoming port elsewhere. Our adventure is not possible without your support.

Vive la Open Access.

Fig. 1. Detail from Hieronymus Bosch, *Ship of Fools* (1490–1500)

DIS/CORD: THINKING SOUND THROUGH AGENTIAL REALISM. Copyright © 2022 by Kevin Toksöz Fairbairn. This work carries a Creative Commons BY-NC-SA 4.0 International license, which means that you are free to copy and redistribute the material in any medium or format, and you may also remix, transform and build upon the material, as long as you clearly attribute the work to the authors (but not in a way that suggests the authors or punctum books endorses you and your work), you do not use this work for commercial gain in any form whatsoever, and that for any remixing and transformation, you distribute your rebuild under the same license. http://creativecommons.org/licenses/by-nc-sa/4.0/

First published in 2022 by punctum books, Earth, Milky Way.
https://punctumbooks.com

ISBN-13: 978-1-68571-046-0 (print)
ISBN-13: 978-1-68571-047-7 (ePDF)

DOI: 10.53288/0360.1.00

LCCN: 2022934994
Library of Congress Cataloging Data is available from the Library of Congress

Book design: Vincent W.J. van Gerven Oei
Cover photograph: Kevin Toksöz Fairbairn

spontaneous acts of scholarly combustion

HIC SVNT MONSTRA

dis/cord

Thinking Sound through Agential Realism

Kevin Toksöz Fairbairn

Contents

Introduction 15

1 ay neden şeftali gibi kokuyor? 25
2 flotsam 55
3 jetsam 77
4 encyclical 97
5 honewort 119

Bibliography 137

Acknowledgments

This book would never have existed without the belief, support, and patience of Marcel Cobussen, Viola Yip, Michael Baldwin, and Brenda Fairbairn. Their care with early drafts of the text were transformative, and this book would not have been possible without their thoughtful conversations about sound, music, and life.

Curtis Rumrill's energy and enthusiasm helped launch this project, and his diligence and kindness in mastering the audio were essential in bringing it to a conclusion.

Many thanks to punctum books: Emma Regeni, for her care and patience with this text, and especially Vincent W.J. van Gerven Oei, whose dedication and persistence made everything possible.

More than anything, I am forever grateful to Işıl Toksöz, whose curiosity and insight allow me to hear the world. You brought so many of these sounds and thoughts to life. For your infinite creativity and incomparable sensitivity, this book is for you.

This work uses embedded audio files throughout, with one work paired to each chapter. The relevant audio examples may be found at the following online repository:

https://www.researchcatalogue.net/view/884924/884925

Introduction

Thinking sound is an activity. Thinking with sound; thinking about sound; thinking through sound: these are all modalities of living with sound as a physical, vibrating reality. Because sound is matter in motion — resonating and reverberating — it resists conceptualization as an object or as a static concept. It cannot be held in a container but rather expends itself in the world, swallowed up by other vibrations and the inertia of matter. It has no body of its own but requires embodiment to exist and propagate. This combination of materiality and ephemerality subverts the documentation of sound and thinking about sound, and instead invites thinking that embraces mutability, motion, and dynamism.

As sound waves radiate out from their source and disperse in the environment, they enact a momentary entanglement of the media and bodies that surround that source, each of which in turn also embody — physically give their bodies to — its sound waves. In interpreting sound, these listening bodies take on special valence. Their ability to respond to sound, whether to enable or obstruct it, provides a real-time conceptualization of sound in its fleeting impermanence. Salomé Voegelin describes this as a "verb-ness" that "invents places and things whose audience is their producer" (Voegelin 2010, 14). Because sound is such a fluid, incorporeal phenomenon, its material reality is produced quite literally by the "audience" of media and bodies in which it reverberates. Thought about in this way, sound "is not interested to linger and hear its outcome. It is perpetually on the move, making time and tenses rather than following them" (ibid.). As it molds the dynamism of time, its spatial reality is constructed by the bodies it encounters, which fabricate it as a material force through their own sympathetic resonance. Sound is "always the heard, immersive and present" (ibid., xiv). Sound's relation to these bodies that comprise the heard is collaborative, for they make sound material. It is sound that "delivers the world in all its materiality while already disappearing into the ether" (LaBelle 2010, 1). But how discrete is the temporal ephemerality of sound? If sound is entangled in these audiating, resonating bodies, then how separable are they? And if they are entangled, then is sound really immaterial? Despite its ephemeral reverberation in the world, is it not still sutured to the bodies that excite its impulse and those that swallow it up as its vibrations die out?

As a sound artist, my journey with sound wanders through a series of parallel corridors: performing music; building and inventing musical instruments; creating sound art and installations; and learning to listen with and through all of these activities. Because thinking with sound orbits around the acts of listening and hearing, the ability to sense looms over everything; perception, though, is by no means guaranteed. Nor is it necessarily a dispassionate act of observation, for sound can also become pain. In my case, as I sense my hearing slowly deteriorate and my tinnitus intensify — even in the course of researching and writing this text — I become increasingly aware of the snaking tendrils of the past that affect and alter both my engagement with sound and my ability to think with, about, and through sound. As my ability to hear irrevocably diminishes, sound itself changes both quantitatively and qualitatively. Deafness is not a lack of perception, nor does an unsensing body necessarily preclude its participation in sounding vibrations. Nonetheless, as my own ability to perceive sound has fundamentally altered over time, I have become increasingly aware of the ways in which sound escapes the confines of the exact moment in which it vibrates, and how an active thinking through sound requires a broader awareness of the material scaffolding in which sounds occur — a scaffolding that stretches discontinuously and disjointedly across spaces and times far removed from any particular sounding moment.

My tinnitus is not just a deterioration of my body; it is also an archive of the experiences that have damaged it. I work with sound every day, and so even as my tinnitus disrupts my ability to do that work, it is also a product of that work. I am not losing my hearing arbitrarily, but precisely because of my relationship to sound as a performer, craftsman, and artist. It is those sounds that have changed me. The musics I have made and the tools I have used produced sounds that nourished my tinnitus. This pain has grown organically from a combination of particularly damaging sounds that I have consistently and repeatedly produced (or exposed myself to), as well as from the steady, unrelenting accrual of those sounds in my body. However, even as this condition has taken a toll on my ability to engage with sound, it has also shown me a new way of working with and thinking through sound. It has made it impossible for me to conceptualize the materiality of a sonic vibration without acknowledging the sea of seemingly unrelated sounds arrayed around it in space and time. I cannot think about a sound I hear today without also considering the vast web of other sounds I've experienced in the past that predict and predicate what and how I can hear today.

In thinking about the materialist aspects of sound, it is easy to become distracted by the immersive holism of its vibration in the sounding moment. Unfortunately, the gravity exerted by this mentality masks the importance of other influences far removed from the sounding moment. There is no definitive cause-and-effect relationship between a noisy tool I used ten years ago and my ability to rehearse with a musical colleague today, and it is impossible to measure exactly how that tool left marks on my body and how that has affected me as a musician today. Nonetheless, these untraceable affective forces accumulate. Despite their resistance to cataloguing, they have an outsize influence on how bodies resonate, respond, and interact with sounds and with each other. Any account of sonic materialism must register these myriad affective events and agencies. The allure of sonic materialism lies in its realism, which is to say, in the idea that sound is not a metaphor but a pulsating force that acts and is acted upon in the world. That picture, though, is drastically incomplete without the threads of entangled influence that stretch backwards in time and space to the forces that have shaped the conditions in which sounds and their perception emerge today.

Christoph Cox describes some of these elements in his concept of a "sonic flux" (Cox 2018, 2), which envisions the "aesthetic simultaneity" of time and space across history. For Cox, sound can be used to imagine "all nature and culture as a collection of flows" (ibid., 3), supporting a materialism in which "all entities and events in the universe are the products of immanent and contingent material and energetic processes" (ibid., 6). While this sonic flux accounts for the entanglement of sounding bodies across space and time, it also threatens to reduce the messiness and complication of that aspatiotemporality, reducing it to a flat dimensionality in which the immanence of sound appears clean and universal. In reality, the continuity of sonic materialism across space and time is characterized as much by disjunction and disruption as it is by resonance and reverberation.

The appeal to immanence also opens up sonic materialism to critique. In apotheosizing the immersive qualities of immanent sound, such appeals risk diluting the realism of their approach in the quasi-mystical celebration of sound as a spherical, boundary-dissolving force outside the linear constraints of visual discourse. Jonathan Sterne refers to this as the "audiovisual litany" (Sterne 2003, 15), referring to thinkers who seek to position sound as a corrective to the binarism and hierarchism inherent in visuality. For Sterne, the construction of immersive, immanent sound is "a false transcendence" (ibid., 19), exaggerating the remediation that the "affect" of "spherical" sound can provide to the "intellect" of "directional" visuality (ibid., 15). He asserts that this false binary contrasting sound and vision is "essentially a restatement of the longstanding spirit/letter distinction in Christian spiritualism" (ibid., 16). His 'audiovisual litany' describes a sonic materialism dependent on the idea that "sound embodies an originary metaphysical immediacy or 'presence' that words and images deny" (James 2019, 3). These forms of materialism rely on a universalism suggesting that "sound embodies material immediacy" (ibid., 4).

It is easy to romanticize sonic materiality as a vibrating force. After all, it has no body of its own, and yet is embodied by everything in its environment — all vibrating in sympathetic resonance or interference. It radiates, producing an immersive field and inviting listeners to engage with this spatial awareness. However, this romanticization belies the messy reality of how sound actually materializes. Sonic materialism is not a continuous flow of undifferentiated vibration. There is no universal reverberation, only the constant murmuring on an infinite multitude of peripherally situated sounds and bodies, contaminating one another in imbalanced disequilibrium. Whether intentionally or unintentionally, these romanticizations reinforce a centrality of sound as it radiates out into the world. Even the word radiation implies a certain privileged locus within a concentric sphere of affectivity. But as I demonstrated by examining the effects of tinnitus, the radiation of sound is a liminal and messy affair. Some forces exert wide influences across discontinuous temporal and spatial planes and, moreover, do not expend themselves in that influence, rather accruing and even intensifying. While the spherical radiation of sound suggests an egalitarianism, the reality is quite different, with the materializations of that radiation reflecting stark and unpredictable imbalance at every scale.

Immersive immanence and disjointed aspatiotemporal entanglement are not mutually exclusive, though. In formulating what she calls "agential realism," Karen Barad attempts to resolve a very similar dissonance. She approaches questions ranging from mundane daily life to metaphysics and ethics by mining her expertise in quantum physics. Although at first glance quantum physics may seem an exotic source, it is in fact highly suited to deal with such a mixture of material and theoretical concerns. Quantum physics requires a constant interplay between theoretical and experimental research methods, both of which depend upon and enrich one another. As such, it serves as an apt framework for developing similar register- and scale-shifting approaches in other fields.

For Barad specifically, the quantum world helps to reveal a dynamism and fluidity inherent in matter that is at odds with classical physics and metaphysics (which observe the world as a series of discrete objects or entities that affect or are affected by one another). Barad's realism requires understanding how matter comes to be in the world, and as a quantum physicist, she is well placed to relate how this occurs on that fundamental scale. In place of a classical conception of pre-existing objects that interact as they encounter one another, Barad proposes a complete reconception of how matter actually materializes. Rather than drawing from a finite well of existing matter, she describes a worldview in which the relations between particles of matter pre-exist their materialization, enabling the concatenation of particles that then come to be in the world. It is not matter itself that exists, but the relations between particles of matter that come together to collaboratively enact their existence. "The primary ontological unit is not independent objects with inherent boundaries and properties but rather *phenomena*" (Barad 2007, 139). Particles come to be *through* their mutual relationships, not as independent objects that collide once and only once they are already in the world. To describe the way in which particles coalesce to co-constitute the world, Barad introduces the term intra-action. "The notion of *intra-action* (in contrast to the usual 'interaction,' which presumes the prior existence of independent entities/relata) represents a profound conceptual shift. It is through specific agential intra-actions that the boundaries and properties of the 'components' of phenomena become determinate" (Barad 2003, 815).

Although the concept of intra-action privileges the entanglement of multiple agencies over the individuality of each agent, it does not implicate all agencies equally. Notably, it eschews the impulse to view this interdependence as an all-encompassing, flat ontology. On the contrary, Barad describes the moment in which particles materialize as an agential cut, which "enacts a *local* resolution *within* the phenomenon of the inherent ontological indeterminacy" (Barad 2003, 815). This agential cut cuts across space and time, allowing multiple agencies at variable removes to become implicated (or not) as the vast sea of potential intra-actions collapses into just one single intra-action. This cut enacts which agencies end up being stitched together and which do not. The terminology of cutting implies that there is not always a clean correlation between spatiotemporal proximity and intra-active entanglement. Rather, intra-active "'emergence' is […] dependent on the nonlinearity of relations" (Barad 2007, 393). The continuity of time and space can be radically fragmented and rearranged "as some things come to matter and others are excluded, as possibilities are opened up and others are foreclosed" (ibid.). Reality itself is continuous, as particles materialize and persist in space and time, but this continuity is made possible by a dynamic interwoven discontinuity, through which a complex entanglement of bodies provides the agential scaffolding that enables specific "relata-within-phenomena [to] emerge through specific intra-actions" (ibid., 815). Matter is not concrete or discrete, but fluid and dynamic. It is an entangled web of agencies at various scales of proximity that enable their mutual emergence. "[M]atter is not a fixed essence; rather, matter is substance in its intra-active becoming" (ibid., 183).

The consubstantiality of seemingly irreconcilable qualities such as continuity and discontinuity are a crucial component of agential realism:

> This strange quantum causality entails the disruption of discontinuity/continuity, a disruption so destabilising, so downright dizzying, that it is difficult to believe that it is that which makes for the stability of existence itself. Or rather, to put it a bit more precisely, if the indeterminate nature of existence by its nature teeters on the cusp of stability and instability, of possibility and impossibility, then the dynamic relation-

ality between continuity and discontinuity is crucial to the open ended becoming of the world which resists acausality as much as determinism. (Barad 2010, 248)

The disruptions that Barad describes are both "joins and disjoins — cutting together/apart — not separate consecutive activities" (ibid., 244). That inseparability implies a form of simultaneity as well: "The point is not merely that something is here-now and there-then without ever having been anywhere in between, it's that here-now, there-then have become unmoored — there's no given place or time for them to be" (ibid., 247–48). Determinacy and indeterminacy are not just interwoven, they are very concretely *entangled*. Barad often resorts to a grammatical slash to conjure the flickering coexistence and interdependence of seemingly oppositional concepts, such as the "in/determinacy at the heart of matter" (Barad 2012, 9). The interwoven fabric of these coextensive inversions are part of the conceptual and material nonlinearity of agential realism, which she describes as a "dis/continuity": "A repetition not of what comes before, or after, but a disruption of before/after. A cut that is itself cross-cut. A cut raised to a higher power forever repeating. A passable impassability" (Barad 2010, 248).

In the passage above, Barad also highlights how recognizing the in/determinate and dis/continuous aspects of reality helps bridge the divide between acausality and determinism. This mirrors the questions raised earlier about sound. Does acknowledging sound's material significance require embracing it as a holistic, immersive presence? Or can there be a similar in/determinacy and dis/continuity to the way in which sound waves entangle with the world, cutting through space and time to splice bodies together in mutual, collaborative entanglement? The immanence of sound belies the disjointed messiness with which it enacts these agential cuts, but it is precisely the unpredictability of that messiness that merits attention. As Barad urges, "the unknown, the insensible, new realms of in/determinacy, which have incalculable effects on mattering, need to be acknowledged, or, even better, taken into account" (Barad 2012, 6–7).

In writing about the un/sympathetic vibration of sound in music, sound art, and life in general, I have sought to capture the ruptured concord and discord that fuses bodies together in the momentary entanglement when sound waves are produced. This dis/cord — a fusion of that consubstantial concord and discord — outlines the necessary messiness that agential realism uses to make sense of the world and the bodies that share space within it. Using agential realism as a framework for examining the entanglement of sound is neither an appeal to scientist positivism nor a reworking of sound's mystical holism. Instead, it is simply an account of the disjointed commingling of bodies in space as they affect each other sonically. It takes stock of the entanglements that already exist — splicing and suturing time and space — and examines the dis/cordant phenomena by which we touch and are touched through sound. Producing sound and experiencing sound become means of thinking with and through other bodies.

Dis/cord also reminds us that, while discourse around sound often circles sympathetic resonance and amplification, it must equally reckon with interference. As I alluded to with my tinnitus, even a life devoted to producing and experiencing beauty in sound art is also entangled with the scars and pain that are threaded through the dis/cordant experience of sound. However, even though this pain helps foreground the elements of sonic entanglement that benefit most from an agential realist perspective, a Baradian approach is equally well suited to the sympathetic resonances and reverberations of music and sound art. Before approaching the body itself, this book will begin with a more patient exploration of Barad's ideas as applied to a piece of notated music, *ay neden şeftali gibi kokuyor?* This piece of music provides a relatively small-scale, self-contained situation in which an agential realist approach to music interpretation can begin to unfold. *flotsam* uses a more experimental piece of music to explore Barad's concepts of touch and self-touch and their materialist resonances with sound. *flotsam*'s partner piece, *jet-*

sam, then approaches Barad's concept of the apparatus and the entanglement of observation, allowing a more dis/continuous conception of listening to emerge. This approach is then further expanded through an account of the sound installation piece *encyclical,* which enacts dis/junctions between the acts of instrument building, performing, and listening. These reflections are then filtered through the body and its scars by a final piece of sound art, *honewort,* which begins and ends within my body while opening it up to the dis/cordant choir of other entities that join it in a vast web of agential realist entanglement.

1

ay neden şeftali gibi kokuyor?

> An uncanny topology: no smooth surfaces, willies everywhere. Differences percolate through every 'thing', reworking and being reworked through reiterative reconfigurings of spacetimematterings — the ongoing rematerialisings of relationalities, not among pre-existing bits of matter in a pre-existing space and time, but in the ongoing reworkings of 'moments', 'places', and 'things' — each being (re)threaded through the other.
> — Barad 2010, 244

I remember very distinctly my first encounter with this passage from Karen Barad, read on a bottom-of-the-line smartphone while standing on a 57A bus transporting me to a rehearsal in Vienna's fifteenth district. Once there, I would join my colleagues in preparing a series of new compositions — some not yet finished — composed for the ensemble's inaugural concert. Time was short and the composers' stress over their unfinished pieces was matched only by the performers' impatience with those composers' yes-yes-definitely-by-tomorrow promises. The whole situation was breathless but hyper-focused, and perhaps discovering Barad's work in such close proximity to such an intensely focused collaborative working process helps explain her transformative effect on me. On this particular day in which I first read the passage above, my curiosity was sufficiently piqued by the end of the rehearsal that I had downloaded some other readily available PDFs of her work to squint at on the bumpy bus ride home. That alone, though, is no great surprise; after all, I, like any other bibliophile in the world, have always been prone to binging on newly discovered writers and thinkers. More startling to me was the indelible and irrevocable effect that these works had on my relationship to working with musicians, with compositions, with instruments, and with sound itself.

A freelance musician's life has a curious metabolism: constantly encountering new creative projects, working intensely on them for short periods, and then moving on and refocusing as new projects beckon. With the exception of the oneiric repetition that is the unique world of touring, most projects fall into roughly five to ten day cycles. Preparation for that particular project intensifies within that period, and for these days one encounters the same people each day, all while the next projects percolate beneath, as one prepares for them mentally and physically in hotel rooms, trains, and airports. One project will occupy the bulk of a performer's attention and energy for this brief period, but these expenditures are always overlaid by the slowly accruing preparation for subsequent projects, which are then in turn accompanied by the preparation for the next. Learning to gauge the time and energy these superposed concentrations require is the one truly necessary skill for a freelancer. These cycles are strange, though. A week or so is a long time to be single-mindedly committed to a specific goal, especially when these efforts are augmented by colleagues and camaraderie; and yet, a week is also a very short time, easily swallowed up by the fog of memory at the remove of even a few weeks. This strange cocktail of intensity and ephemerality produces strange patterns of consciousness and memory. I could not tell you precisely which projects preceded or succeeded the concert at Vienna's *Echoraum* which accompanied my first forays into Barad's agential realism, and yet the paradigm shift that her work enacted within my personal consciousness renders this singular project distinctly vivid in my recollection.

Barad's agential realism introduces a terminology and discourse that is especially ripe for interdisciplinary borrowing. As a practicing musician, I seized at first upon some of the metaphorical possibilities, especially her use of diffraction, following the work of Donna Haraway. She proposes it as an alternative form of critique, advocating a "practice of diffraction, of reading diffractively for patterns of differences that make a difference" (Barad in Dolphijn and van der Tuin 2012, 49). As a musician specialized in performing contemporary and experimental music, this immediately interested me, as its application could fundamentally upend more traditional conceptions of the composer–performer–audience hierarchy. Searching for "patterns of differences that make a difference" stresses how different agents at different points in the creative process can influence and warp each other's work in a collaborative rather than conflictual way. Musicians tend to treat composers' agency (and fidelity to the text) and performers' agency (interpretive flexibility) as opposite ends of a binary spectrum, almost as though they each draw from a finite well of creative potential. This makes the interpretation of music a linear process, in which a composers' vision initiates a process which can be honored, diverted, or even hijacked by a performers' interpretive liberty or an audience members' impression or analysis. Music becomes a hermeneutic tug-of-war, in which independent distortions accrue in a linear progression.

Thinking of diffraction as a process of interacting with scores or producing musical criticism provides an alternative to this mentality, though. Rather than a temporally bound conveyor belt in which each step of the process simply adds or subtracts to the previous one, diffraction subjects that linear progression to a slew of refractive possibilities. Interpretation affects the text, but not as a heavy-handed imposition; rather, interpretation enters a diffractive relationship in which both composer and interpreter are affected and transformed by each other's interpolations. As Barad makes clear, diffraction describes an interaction that does not subtract agency from one site in order to reapportion it elsewhere. Instead, the linear becomes panoramic, omnidirectional. Diffractive readings allow for loci of creativity (e.g., composers, interpreters) to exist while still welcoming agency from liminal, peripheral elements. This provides a way to conceive of performer and audience agency (not to mention other, nonanthropocentric players) that opens up the creative process to their diffractive potential without creating a binary opposition to composers. Barad uses diffraction to harness the creative potential of a rich, panoramic field of entangled agencies, celebrating that potential without subtracting or deconstructing other voices to make that possible. This is a rather superficial gloss of diffraction, though. While using the concept of diffraction as a metaphor to conceptualize a more complex relationship of mutual creative influence may help the scales fall from the eyes of classically trained musicians like myself, its potential importance as a tool for thinking about music is far more nuanced.

Haraway's own understanding of the concept, derived from classical physics, explores the roles of superposition, refraction, and interference as tools for critical inquiry, as well as for simply coexisting with and relating to others. Approaching the idea for the first time, Haraway quotes Trinh Minh-ha's formulation of the "inappropriate/d others" (Trinh 1986/7, 3), asserting that "'inappropriate/d' does not mean 'not to be in relation with,'" but rather "to be in critical, deconstructive relationality, in a diffracting rather than reflecting" (Haraway 1992, 69). It is "the means of making potent connection that exceeds domination" (ibid.). In contrasting diffracting to reflecting, Haraway attempts to evoke a paradigm shift in thinking, such that otherness is situated and complicit rather than in binary opposition (to something nominally not-other). Diffraction evokes a relationality that can shift from vantage point to vantage point, or from one point in time to another. That mutability becomes both an advantage and a goal. As Haraway notes, "Trinh was looking for a way to figure 'difference' as a 'critical difference within,' and not as special taxonomic marks grounding difference as apartheid" (ibid., 70). Critically, the "within" that Trinh and Haraway describe is a concatenation of multiples others, mutually complicit and cooperative. Diffraction celebrates the potential energy implicit in otherness, welcoming the distortions and reimaginations that multiple bodies or agencies can provoke in each other through their mutual diffraction.

In embarking from Haraway's use of diffraction, Barad opens up an additional dimension of the term, even further reducing the elements of difference between others: "Diffraction, understood using quantum physics, is not just a matter of interference, but of entanglement [...]. This difference is very important. It underlines the fact that knowing is a direct material engagement, a cutting together-apart, where cuts do violence but also open up and rework the agential conditions of possibility" (Barad in Dolphijn and van der Tuin 2012, 52). As a metaphorical tool, diffraction encourages dialogue and interactivity, but for both Haraway and Barad, diffraction also shifts registers between the theoretical and the material. In addition to being useful as a conceptual tool, it also maps the very literal interdependence of material bodies and objects in the world (an interdependence that takes on special valence in the quantum world that Barad studies). It encourages a creative process that enables a diversity of voices and assimilates the creative energy of all types and scales of agents, human and nonhuman, at all points in the process. Barad stresses the scientific realism of diffraction, stressing that the material reality of this entanglement has serious ramifications for the bodies and objects implicated: "Objectivity, instead of being about offering an undistorted mirror image of the world, is about accountability to marks on bodies, and responsibility to the entanglements of which we are a part" (ibid.).

While metaphorical interpretive tools plucked from philosophy or science may be flush with creative potential, they are hardly unique phenomena. There are fertile metaphorical and conceptual tools around every corner, it sometimes seems, and scholars in the arts are rarely shy about appropriating them. Agential realism seemed to offer something else, though. It didn't seek enlightenment, but entanglement, and any emergence of the former remained coincidental to the latter. Thinking about nonhuman agency in the creative production of sound boiled down, inevitably and necessarily, to Barad's literal marks on bodies and their entangled topography of ephemeral, interlaced agencies. By scaling out from textual hermeneutics to corporeality, Barad's diffractive entanglement acknowledged the extremely physical (and emotional) expenditures of music-making. For all of its intellectual rigor, the legacy of *Werktreue* and the composer–performer hierarchy in Western art music occlude the unavoidable fact that instrumentalism (vocalizing especially) is an embodied phenomenon. Music is made by bodies in space and time, and no extravagance of intellectual rigor can supplant that.

In conventional notated music, this can mean many things. Diffraction makes it easier to account for the role that a musical instrument, for example, can play in the creative process. The concerns of the performer's body (both its virtuosity as well as its limitations) typically elicit more attention than the instrument itself—albeit while still remaining secondary to compositional intent. This is not always the case, as evidenced in particular compositional developments spurred on or even dictated by technological advances in instrumental design. However, those anomalies serve to demonstrate the point, for if instruments only breach the surface of musicological discourse in these moments of exception, and even then only as muses to a larger creative vision, that merely underscores their otherwise irrelevance. By contrast, thinking music through diffraction and entanglement explodes this seeming inconsequentiality of musical instruments, helping to reveal the creative process as a larger, nonlinear panorama of time and space. So long as a musical instrument is an afterthought to composition, the idea of a linear progression from composition to performance can be maintained, but the moment that decisions in instrument construction are acknowledged as elements of the creative process (some taking place years or decades before a piece of music is composed), this linearity collapses. A musical instrument may still serve primarily as a support to composition rather than a driver of it, but its interpolations in the creative process are stutteringly atemporal, with decades-old designs gaining unexpected valence and cutting open and across the creative possibilities of a musical collaboration.

Instruments contain a host of their own concerns: idiomaticism of technique; projection in space; the ability to blend with other instruments; the physical relationship to the performer (demands of stamina, extended techniques, etc.); the availability for compositional experimentation; ease of transport; audibility to the listener; the list goes on and on. Once again, if taken as a displacement of agency from a composer (or performer, whomever or whatever), this sets up unnecessary binary oppositions. However, if an immersive entanglement of agencies is taken seriously, these instrumental concerns very quickly contaminate all other compositional, rehearsal, and performance situations. The interweaving overtakes the individual strands, a point Barad emphasizes, asserting that it is in fact the interweaving which defines and makes possible the individual strands. She writes, "'Distinct' agencies are only distinct in a relational, not an absolute sense, that is, agencies are only distinct in relation to their mutual entanglement; they don't exist as individual elements" (Barad 2010, 267). If agents are not discrete in a traditional sense, then their diffractive superposition cannot be conflictual, irrespective of the quality of their coming-together, whether it be mutual interference or amplification or anything in between. In a quantum world, Barad describes this phenomenon as *intra-action*:

> The notion of *intra-action* (in contrast to the usual 'inter-action,' which presumes the prior existence of independent entities/relata) represents a profound conceptual shift. It is through specific agential intra-actions that the boundaries and properties of the 'components' of phenomena become determinate and that particular embodied concepts become meaningful. A specific intra-action [...] enacts an *agential cut* (in contrast to the Cartesian cut — an inherent distinction — between subject and object) effecting a separation between 'subject' and 'object.' That is, the agential cut en-

acts a *local* resolution *within* the phenomenon of the inherent ontological indeterminacy. In other words, relata do not preexist relations; rather, relata-within-phenomena emerge through specific intra-actions. Crucially then, intra-actions enact *agential separability* — the local condition of *exteriority-within-phenomena*. (Barad 2003, 815)

The agential cut represents a particular moment, a phenomenon in which a variety of agents coalesce — "a congealing of agency" (Barad 2007, 184) — through their mutual co-constitution. They are interdependent, in a sense inseparable, instantiating an indeterminacy only locally resolved in a particular moment. "There are no separately determinate individual entities that interact with one another; rather, the co-constitution of determinately bounded and propertied entities results from specific intra-actions" (Barad 2010, 253). Barad's language revels in these flickering irresolutions and (seeming) contradictions, just as the electrons in the quantum world she describes, existing not in spite of but because of their indeterminacy. She describes the indeterminate consubstantiality of binaries that would, in a more classical context, be considered diametrically opposed:

> There is no fixed dividing line between 'self' and 'other', 'past' and 'present' and 'future', 'here' and 'now', 'cause' and 'effect'. Quantum discontinuity is no ordinary disjunction. Cartesian cuts are undone. Agential cuts, by contrast, do not mark some absolute separation but a cutting together/apart — a 'holding together' of the disparate itself, […] without wounding the dis-jointure, the dispersion, or the difference, without effacing the heterogeneity of the other […] without or before the synthetic junction of the conjunction and the disjunction. (ibid., 265)

"This 'collapse' — or rather, resolution — of an ontological/hauntological indeterminacy into a determinate state" (ibid., 251) is the agential cut, whereby a particular set of localized determinacies and agents emerge through their interlaced being-in-the-world. "Agential cuts — intra-actions — don't produce (absolute) separation, they engage in agential separability — differentiating and entangling (that's one move, not successive processes). Agential cuts radically rework relations of joining and disjoining." (ibid., 265). This interplay between both the joined and the disjoined enables this conceptual framework to serve as more than just a metaphor for the collision of agents in the world, a quasi-spiritual immersive holism at work despite the apparent fragmentation of our environment. In an intra-active understanding of the constant (re)constitution of identity and agency in the world, the dance between "joining and disjoining" reflects the simultaneity of both perceived and actual fragmentations and holisms. Agential separability enables the language of fragmentation while still acknowledging the ontological interdependency from which that separability is molded.

It is important to remember that Barad is describing real-world phenomena, not thought experiments or philosophical speculations. Metaphorically rich though diffraction and intra-action may be, they describe the actual quantum reality of the world around us. In filtering these ideas through artistic practice, their intermingled reality and conceptualism offer complementary tools. The language and terminology that intra-action offers supports an engagement with the creative process that celebrates the collision and commingling of agencies throughout the process. As one of many potential examples, I have chosen to focus on the musical instrument itself, although any other element or parameter could serve equally well. In my first, rudimentary application of these ideas, I was performing a duo for trombone and cello by Santiago Díez-Fischer. The instrument — in this case a trombone — played a unique role in bridging temporal and spatial divides within the compositional process. Díez-Fischer, living in a separate country, bought a cheap trombone and began working with it himself, completely untrained. This is no abnormal occurrence within the contemporary classical music world, especially with string and percussion instruments. In experimenting with the trombone, he found a large palette of noisy, grainy, spittly sounds lurking on

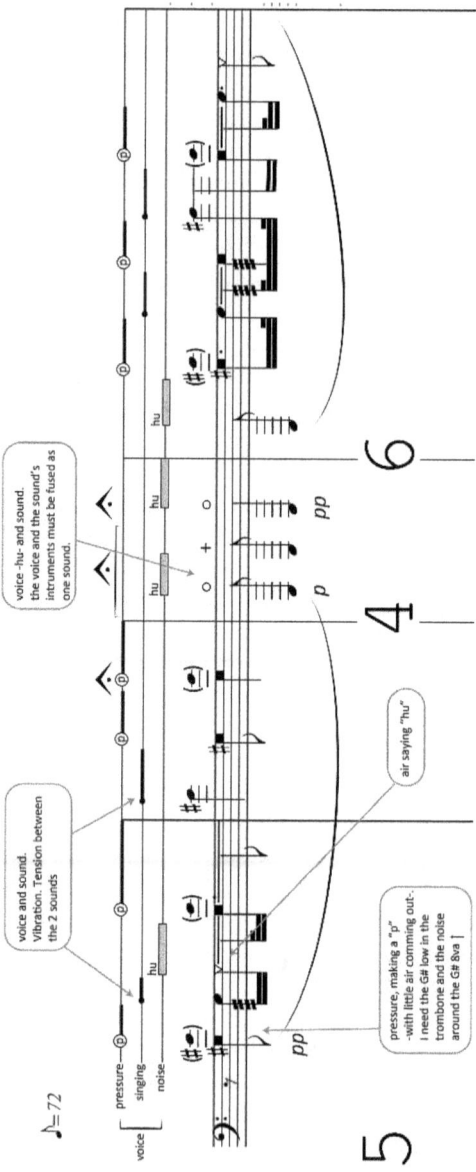

Fig. 1. Sketch for Santiago Díez-Fischer, *sensitive switch* (2015). Reprinted with permission.

the periphery of normal pitches (were one to play the trombone in a traditional classical style). These sounds — though Díez-Fischer did not discover them alone and they have been well and often used in avant-garde music both composed and improvised — lend themselves to the technique of a beginner or non-specialist. Rather than focusing on traditional pitches and rhythms, Díez-Fischer explored these liminal terrains within the potential sound world made possible by how a trombone is played: namely, by a human body compressing air from their lungs through two fleshy lips into a giant metal megaphone.

Díez-Fischer proceeded to map these possibilities in a two-dimensional notation. The first versions of the notation that Díez-Fischer sent me included a mix of traditional pitch-based notation and a tablature of other physical actions that produced (or obscured) the resultant sound (fig. 1).

The upper staff indicates three types of sound production, each using a different body part: lips, oral cavity, vocal cords. The pitch notation is traditional, with parenthetical notes alluding to some of the coincidental pitch material that results from the superposition of normal played notes and the other three forms of sound production indicated above. Because the pitches bridge the gaps between notes and techniques, and because the different forms of sound production require unique bodily configurations, the resultant sound is a shifting tapestry of effects with relatively smooth, gradated transitions from timbre to timbre. Each combination of overlaid techniques produces a new angle, a new perspective within the panoramic realm of what sound a human and a trombone can collectively produce. The fact that the pitches stay primarily consistent, hovering around G#'s in different octaves, lends the whole passage a kaleidoscopic effect, as though the instrument, the performer, and the listener are orbiting each other in a multi-dimensional space, each sound representing a slightly altered view and vantage point of the same phenomenon within its field of potential.

Following this sketch, Díez-Fischer and I communicated via recordings, email, and video chat, discovering the idiosyncrasies of his and my own expressions of these various techniques

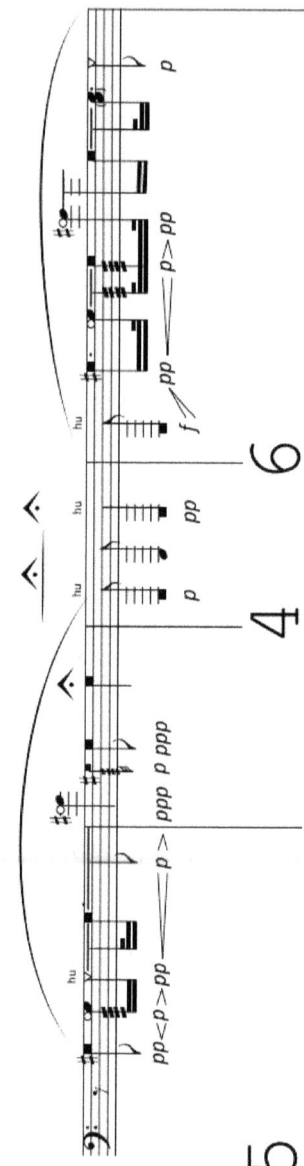

Fig. 2. Measures 1–4 from Santiago Díez-Fischer, *sensitive switch* (2015). Reprinted with permission.

and their superposition in the performing and instrumental body. Some effects worked radically differently for him with his new trombone (and his rather fresh relationship to it) than for me and my trombone (and my comparably ancient history with my old hunk of metal). Eventually, Díez-Fischer compressed the notation into a single stream of information that contained hints of each of the previous four strands of information. Interestingly, while the sonic result is the same, the final notation (fig. 2) elides visual representation of the interaction and gradation of sounds that is more readily appreciable in the previous, tablaturized version. Although it streamlines information and is far easier to read, it gives a somewhat misleading impression of blocks of discrete sounds following one another, belying the melting and shimmering effects of the actual sounding result. The instrumental technique described by this music notation is inextricably entangled with the empirical trajectory of its genesis, with the accrued embodied knowledges of two different human bodies and two different trombones, on varying timescales and in multiple cities. In a sense, the final notated version documents this processual unfolding as much or more than the musical result that it prescribes.

This notation, however, only comprises half of the trombone part in the piece. The second half requires the trombonist to play a bassoon reed in the trombone, producing a radically different timbre, if equally noisy. As with the vocabulary of techniques explored in the sketch above, using a bassoon reed in the trombone is far from a new invention for this piece. In fact, Díez-Fischer utilized it in large part because of his familiarity with my previous work using woodwind reeds and mouthpieces (bassoon, saxophone, clarinet, etc.) in the trombone. While infrequently asked for, it is a standard technique in contemporary classical and avant-garde musics, especially in the twenty-first century. However, although most trombonists literate in this repertoire have access to a bassoon reed and have had occasion to perform with one, few spend much time practicing with such reeds on a regular basis. As it happens, I did (and still do), and consider these augmentations of the instrument a major part of my instrumental technique. While the first half of the piece explored sounds primarily derived from Díez-Fischer's personal explorations of untrained (in the best possible way!) trombone technique, the latter half takes advantage of a specific predilection afforded by the presence of a particular performer.[1]

Taken as a whole, the piece presents a twinned unfolding of investigations and experiments performed by two different people over a variety of time scales: years, months, days, and in some cases hours. The disparate entanglements we each experienced through our relationships with multiple trombones (and bassoons) unfurled into the distinct sound world of the piece. These complex interminglings of agency continued in the course of rehearsals. Heretofore, I have only touched on the particular aspects of the creative process triggered or filtered through the trombone, but there was one other instrument in the mix. As it was not my purview, I will refrain from a similarly detailed discussion of the cello technique in the piece, but will nonetheless relate portions of the working process in which its presence came to bear on the issues already discussed.

As with most pieces of experimental new music, the rehearsal process is a laboratory, in this case for investigating the superposition of instrumental techniques and timbres. Having written an equally experimental cello part for the piece *sensitive switch,* Díez-Fischer joined myself and cellist Myriam García-Fidalgo by video for rehearsals, as well as offering feedback on recordings we made during the week. In the cases of both halves of the piece discussed above, the superposition of distinctive trombone timbres with the cello required adaptation. Both dynamic levels and timbral mixtures required we, as performers,

---

[1] Interestingly, Díez-Fischer changed this effect for the second trombonist who performed the piece. Although the other performer is also very proficient with bassoon reed, Díez-Fischer instead utilized an electronic effect that mimicked the same timbre, in this case drawing on a particular specialty and body of work of the performer in question (Weston Olencki). His willingness to tailor the piece to reflect the personal practices and curiosities of individual performers resonates strongly with the discussion at hand.

and Díez-Fischer in his home in another city, to make decisions about just how these superpositions ought to sound. We proceeded as though we were rotating a three-dimensional object looking for the perfect angle to showcase a particular profile, consulting each other's aural impressions and taking note of the idiosyncratic acoustic profile of the concert venue in an attempt to optimize the entanglement of our respective instrumental practices — only we were physically inside the object we were manipulating, not external to it.

Similar musical problems are solved every day all over the world, and they do not necessarily demand or require any particular conceptual framework or methodology. On the contrary, the diversity of practical and philosophical approaches of the multitude of musicians and artists engaged in these pursuits is itself a beautiful, entangled polyphony. But this particular experience was an initial foray into deliberately choosing diffractive and intra-active tools to help resolve the musical conundrums we faced. Because Díez-Fischer's piece makes such extensive use of a highly individualized instrumental technique, the creative process is already cut open to reveal extensive threads of activity across highly disparate times and spaces. The compositional process, as it were, is not confined to a singular man seated at his writing desk and translating the fantasies of his imagination onto a blank white page. What would this compositional process be without Díez-Fischer's trip to a music store to find a cheap trombone?[2] Or without the exchange of recordings and videos documenting our respective relationships with the in-

---

2 Díez-Fischer's purchase of a cheap, experimental trombone opens up a whole other web of influences rippling outwards in the creative process. Díez-Fischer is far from the only composer to buy cheap instruments to help them compose, and a comparison would show just how impactful the particular instruments found can be, as the quality of the instrument can have a huge effect on the music that emerges downstream. For example, while Díez-Fischer's trombone was in fairly good shape, I also received a different piece in that time period from a composer who had worked with a trombone in very poor condition. Having composed with a trombone slide that barely moved, the composer incorporated that jerkiness of slide motion into the harmonic and timbral language of the piece, forcing me

strument? Or, for that matter, without the previous years I had spent practicing, composing, and recording pieces for trombone with bassoon reed? Each of these disparate experiences and interactions are enmeshed in the process through which the piece emerged. None alone dictated the piece's final form, but their influences on each other are inextricably entangled. It is impossible to point at one particular aspect of the piece and describe with confidence its provenance. Even as we rehearsed, we had to continually consult the individual histories with the trombone of both Díez-Fischer and myself. Even as such a decision is highly subjective, and still tethered to the nominal composer of the piece, Díez-Fischer, it is inextricably caught up in the particular histories of the bodies in question: this performer, this trombone, this reed, this cellist and cello, this microphone, etc.

In using these experiences as a means to stumble into Barad's world, I found that engaging these rehearsal problems diffractively proved highly effective. Acknowledging a larger panorama of agencies all entangled with one another is liberating, but as previously noted, the key difference between a diffractive approach and a more classical one is the shift from seeing disparate agencies as oppositional to seeing them as superpositions, collaboratively engaged in their respective (co)existence. Even if a classical approach does not label, for example, composer and performer agencies as outright oppositions or binaries, their spatial conception is such that they do not overlap. A composer's decision is a composer's decision, and that quickly relegates the performer's role to a purely interpretive one. Viewing their respective agencies as superposed and entangled, on the other hand, welcomes the creative contribution of all of their histories and engagements with one another, with their instruments, with other musics and with other sounds.

My decision-making in investigating the timbral complexity of *sensitive switch* benefitted from this approach, especially

---

to then retroactively mimic the effects of a barely functional trombone on my own instrument which is, for better or for worse, much better cared for.

considering the time constraints within the working process. It would have been easy to subsume my experience with the trombone to Díez-Fischer's, mimicking his own recordings with the trombone and assuming that any timbral or dynamic problems with the cello were just natural consequences of the piece and therefore unresolvable. I could also just as easily have disregarded his work with the instrument, supplanting his experiments with the trombone with my own ideas about how it *should* be done on the instrument, asserting the fact that on this topic I — not Díez-Fischer — am the expert in the room. Instead, I accepted the triangulated superposition of agency between myself, Díez-Fischer, our instruments, and our histories, and mined those entanglements for new sounds and possibilities. Even in the limited time available, I experimented with the polyphonic techniques of Díez-Fischer's tablature notations, finding the grains and bubbles within the sound that helped it to breathe a bit of both of us. I diffracted my own experience with the bassoon reed through Díez-Fischer's imagination and the cellist's technique to find subtle variations that helped to create a quite unique and provocative sounding result. All of these eventualities would have been quite easy to truncate or altogether elide, and perhaps the eventual performance would have been no more or less successful. Nonetheless, experimenting with a diffractive, intra-active approach had appreciable consequences for the unfolding of the creative process, and it left an indelible impression.

The flickering, intertwined agencies of composers to instruments to performers to listeners (and so on) enacted what Barad describes in physics as "cuts [that] rework the [...] conditions of possibility" (Barad in Dolphijn and van der Tuin 2012, 52). I began to think of these agencies intuitively as intra-active, that is, as partners in their mutual co-constitution, "distinct [only] in a relational, not an absolute sense" (Barad 2010, 267). They (and we, and I) become determinate through entanglement, through the unavoidable diffraction of our co-existence. I approached notations looking for the elements of our entanglement that could encourage this "resolution [...] into a determinate state" (ibid., 251). In particular, I found myself returning more and more to her comments that intra-action remains, in the end, "about accountability to marks on bodies" (Barad in Dolphijn and van der Tuin 2012, 52). In the case of Díez-Fischer's piece, the marks on bodies include the various instruments, performers, and paraphernalia that coalesced across time and space in the concert venue, rendering these disparate experiments and simple existences answerable to one another. Barad returns frequently to the neologism response-able, which sums up well my musical reactions to her insistence on our "responsibility to the entanglements of which we are a part" (Barad in ibid.). Writing, learning, and performing music intra-actively entails cultivating this ability to respond, a simple willingness to engage (to entangle), and an understanding that that is non-linear and multi-directional.

In pursuing a sense of response-ability to these marks on bodies, I began to examine the implications of intra-action for the procedures of learning music. Although learning and practicing music are also entangled with the antecedent and subsequent acts of composition and performance, focusing on learning itself acknowledges the input of notation and the output of performance while unfolding within a more malleable timeframe. This is to say that, the arrival of a score and the eventual performance provide useful bookends for organizing one's thinking about learning a piece of music. As previously demonstrated, these temporal landmarks are largely arbitrary, seeing as longer histories of composition and instrumental practice are often at play and first performances rarely serve as the final engagement with a piece or its learning process. These qualifications notwithstanding, the nominally clear outlines of the learning process's score-to-performance timeframe supplied me with a laboratory to explore how a diffractive, intra-active approach could change me as a musician.

While this initially led me to engage thoughtfully with a series of pieces that I approached professionally, it quickly transformed into a much more committed, longterm exploration of the embodiment of instrumental music-making and the response-ability that musicians can show to nonhuman agencies—like instruments and notations. Both instruments and notations are in some ways inseparable from their entanglement with the performing body that holds or reads them, respectively, and yet they are also capable of collaborating response-ably in the generation of new techniques and new forms of instrumental idiomaticism. These investigations provided a large part of my dissertation on the learning process of experimental music notations (such as Díez-Fischer's tablature). Intra-action became a key component of an overall learning methodology that seeks to welcome and accentuate the unique characteristics of each piece, endeavoring to learn much more than just a circumscribed set of prescribed musical gestures, and rather to allow each piece to entangle with my whole history as a trombonist and to teach me new skills and new sounds—all diffracted through my bodily relationship with the trombone and my personal instrumental and performative capacity. Each new piece that I learn is a new opportunity to entangle myself with something unforeseeable, and to participate in the process by which these new conditions enable our mutual "resolution […] into a determinate state" (Barad 2010, 251). Intra-action became part of a larger investigation into embodied cognition and music, as I examined the role that embodied knowledge plays in the development of new techniques and notations. Music emerges from the indeterminate dis- and con-junction of the self and the other, of past and present marks on bodies. Each agent, distinct within its intra-active entanglement, serves only to enable the confluence of notations, creativities, and personalities in specific acoustic performativities.

Barad insists on the intermingling of the philosophical and practical. As previously stressed, for Barad, intra-action is not only a powerful metaphor but first and foremost a description of the reality of the world, moment to moment. To be sure, she is describing events on a quantum level, but as she remarks, the more we learn about the nature of the universe, the less the distinction between micro-level quantum physics and macro-level Newtonian physics holds. Intra-action is a fact of life, not only a useful tool for harnessing embodied cognition for learning music. And sound — although palpable at a macro-scale far removed from the micro-scale of the quantum phenomena Barad normally describes — is also a uniquely suitable medium for exploring the implications of intra-action as both metaphor and reality. Sound waves are, after all, waves that superpose and diffract. Audiation is a physical phenomenon: that we hear sound is a result of the physical vibration of the media in our environment. As humans, our relationship with sound far exceeds the mere imprint of sound waves on our eardrums and our conscious embedding in the world. Vibrations are physical interpolations in the world, and they serve just as easily to enable pain as they do pleasure. Not all music is pastime, as recent literature on the weaponization of sound and music demonstrates, particularly with respect to its uses in torture (cf. Nielsen and Cobussen 2012; Volcler 2013; and Cusick 2013). Intra-action provides a unique means to examine the intersection of media and agencies that are entangled in sound waves and our relationship to them. I have long considered my artistic practice as a sonic rather than a purely musical pursuit. Even as an undergraduate I eschewed labeling my work music and invented in its place the term sonic botany to describe my engagement with the cultivation and documentation of sound in music and beyond. As an artist who has always considered sound itself as the medium in which I work, agential realism posed even greater questions to my more general artistic practice than it did to the isolated study of embodiment and experimental notations.

Interrogating sound through agential realism runs the risk of succumbing to what Barad herself calls "flat-footed analogies between 'macro' and 'micro' worlds" (Barad 2010, 240). Sound waves are far more straightforward than the quantum phenomena she describes, such as the radically fluid wave/particle duality of light. Still, as she herself suggests, the implications of intra-action do merit attention in the macro-realm (cf. Barad 2007, 189–222), and sound provides a useful starting point. To begin with, sound's unique profile as a wave-based, non-visual medium of physical interaction already disorients our perception from the overbearing influence of visuality on our perception. As previously noted, an agential realist account of the environment requires a global awareness, capable of dissolving a linear, subject-object vector of perception into a wider arena of omnidirectional contact and influence. Sound waves effect precisely such a dissolution through their simultaneous directionality within a field of omnidirectional activity. Sound (often) originates from a central point and radiates outwards, lending itself to localized subjectivity in both its instigation and its perception. This threading of agency through the acts of observation and instantiation are crucial to agential realism (and will be examined more fully below), but for now let it suffice to say that sound is not merely a phenomenon constituted by its perception. As the age-old question goes: if a tree falls in the forest and no one is around to hear it, does it still make a sound? This question suggests that a sound's existence depends on the closed circuit from its impulse to its perception, but from the sound waves' perspective, there is no appreciable difference between vibrating through the air or through another tree's living wood than through a human ear canal (or the rest of the human body, for that matter). Sound's existence in the world is defined by this collapse of an extremely directional phenomenon into an omnidirectional field of influence. Even as each different medium — air, skin, wood, water — alters the viscosity of the sound waves' physical manifestation, all of these media still vibrate, both transmitting and undergoing the sonic. Aden Evens describes this onmidirectional sonic field:

> An open E-string bowed on a violin excites at once the string, the body of the violin, the other strings, the body of the violinist, the air around the violin, the material of the room, and the bodies of the listeners. When one wave meets another, they add together, reinforcing each other when they are in phase and canceling each other when they are out of phase. Thus, every sound interacts with all the vibrations already present in the surrounding space; the sound, the total timbre of an instrument is never just that instrument, but that in-

strument in concert with all the other vibrations in the room, other instruments, the creaking of chairs, even the constant, barely perceptible motion of the air. Measured at some point in space, all of this vibration adds up to a continuous variation in pressure, a wave. Complex, irregular, and erratic, this wave changes constantly and incorporates many frequencies and shifting amplitudes. (Evens 2005, 6–7)

Although sound waves enact a more classical form of diffraction than the quantum understanding that Barad invokes, the omnidirectionality that Evens describes — the superposition of media and vibrations saturating a non-hierarchical field — mimics the diffractive character that typifies an intra-active understanding of interlaced agencies. When considering single particles or waves, the apparent linearity of diffraction or refraction subverts an accounting of its intra-activity. Barad cautions that "diffraction is not reflection raised to some higher power. It is not a self-referential glance back at oneself" (Barad 2007, 88). That is to say, diffraction does not describe a single strand tethered on two ends, bridging a divide. Sonic diffraction is not just about the manner in which sound waves' trajectory traverses from a point A to a point B through whatever interferences it encounters. When sound saturates a space, with each point distilling a unique constellation of vibrations and media, the omnidirectional commingling of waves and media enact new sonic phenomena throughout. The sound that reaches point B is not the same sound that emerged from point A. After all, it is not the sound wave itself traveling; each medium vibrates itself, exciting its neighboring media in kind. The vibration of a medium at point B is a localized phenomenon inhering in the physical medium that exists at precisely that point, no matter how intrinsically related to the impulse at point A it may also be. "Relations of exteriority, connectivity, and exclusion are reconfigured. The changing topologies of the world entail an ongoing reworking of the notion of dynamics" (ibid., 141).

Evens underscores that while some sounds may dominate our personal perception, they are inextricably interwoven with a huge diversity of other sound waves and media in our environment. The dynamics at play in an environment of sonically vibrating media enact an omnidirectional, ceaseless superposition and diffraction. The topology of this environment is perpetually dynamic, and the relationship of all the media to each other belies any clear hierarchy of exteriority or connectivity. The texture of the resultant sound is fluid, markedly discrete at all points along both spatial and temporal scales, and yet congealed in their interdependency — ultimately any vacuum breaks the chain of tactile proximity by which each particle and medium transmits and undergoes the sonic morass of intra-acting vibrations. Donna Haraway points out that "a diffraction pattern does not map where differences appear, but rather maps where the effects of differences appear" (Haraway 1992, 300); sound is itself the mapping of such effected difference. The transmission of a sound wave is ultimately immaterial, indifferent. The topology of difference — of superposition and interference and amplification — emerges only through the tactile intra-action of media.

Sound, then, helps to demonstrate on a macro-level one of the most essential tenets of Barad's agential realism, namely, that "matter is not a fixed essence; rather, matter is substance in its intra-active becoming — not a thing but a doing" (Barad 2007, 183–84). In asserting this, Barad counters the atomism of traditional metaphysics, which she describes as a "*Thingification* — the turning of relations into 'things,' 'entities,' 'relata'" (Barad 2003, 812, emphasis in original). She advocates instead a performative understanding of matter, one in which matter participates in its becoming. Her assertions that agency is not exterior to the entanglement of agents may seem radical or even counter-intuitive in the context of Cartesian metaphysics, but as soon as they are thought in relation to a saturated field of sonic activity,[3] they begin to sound intuitive. There is in fact no

---

3   It is useful to reflect on the fact that such a "saturated field of sonic activity" occurs anywhere matter vibrates, and therefore, anywhere there is matter.

such object or agent as a sound or a sound wave, no such *thing*. Sound's existence emerges only in the iterative participation of all surrounding agencies, each complicit and interdependent within this intra-active becoming. Before the casual reader dismisses this observation as pithy or immaterial, I would remind them once more of the traces sound leaves of its presence in the world, of the lingering material evidence of this non-thing with no mass or identity. Sound is physical and it leaves actual marks on bodies, from the violence of trees flattened by a sonic boom or eardrums burst by high amplitude frequencies to the more mundane perturbations of frogsong, transmitted as ripples radiating in a pond. Relationality is not a metaphor. Barad's assertion that matter is not a thing but a doing is an accurate assessment of the diffractive tapestry of intra-activity through which matter becomes, implicated in its own materialization.

This performative understanding of interdependent coming-into-being requires a reimagination of causality. Because of the entire field of spatiotemporal agencies that become entangled with one another, a linear conception of cause and effect breaks down very quickly, replaced instead by innumerable vectors of influence, superposed in relationships of both con- and dis-sonance. Barad writes:

> It is through specific intra-actions that a causal structure is enacted. Intra-actions effect what's real and what's possible, as some things come to matter and others are excluded, as possibilities are opened up and others are foreclosed [...] intra-actions effect the rich topology of connective causal relations that are iteratively performed and reconfigured. (Barad 2007, 393)

Here, the notions of exclusion or foreclosure take on a particular valence. In a linear conception of causality, an effect is the inclusive result of a cause. That is to say, causation is the impulse by which a new element is injected into being — included, as it were, in the world. In Barad's quantum understanding, matter is characterized primarily by its indeterminacy, in that it does not exist external to or prior to its intra-active emergence in the world. Existence is a manner of infinite potentialities, and the agential cut, wherein a conglomeration of agencies congeal in their intra-active becoming, enacts an exclusion of potential rather than an inclusion of identity. For Barad, mattering is an act of coming into existence in the world, an intra-active fusion, and the course by which "some things come to matter and others are excluded" (ibid.) is determined constructively through the diffraction of multitudinous agencies. Rather than a destructive (or deconstructive) form of exclusion, Barad's exclusion is an alternative to the hierarchical determinism of a linear cause and effect, one in which an omnidirectional field of influence converges in the agential enacting of possibility. When she describes the "rich topology of causal relations" (ibid.), she evokes the panoramic field of liminal agencies and influences that augment a nominally causal impulse.

In quantum understanding, these relationships become abundantly rich in spatiotemporal variety. In later chapters I will discuss in more detail experiments that demonstrate the fluid relationship quantum causation has to time (spoiler: causal influence can flow both directions in space and time). At this moment, though, I will simply seek to underline once again the interesting complement that the sonic macro world offers to the quantum micro world. Sound waves are constantly superposed, not only with other waves and static media, but also with their own reflections and refractions. The entire study of acoustics deals with the understanding and manipulation of sound waves in fixed spaces. While the most prevalent discussions of acoustics revolve around rooms (e.g., concert halls, noise barriers on highways), musical instruments also provide a fascinating study of acoustic phenomena in variably closed confines.

The study of sound waves projected into an instrument, vibrating through an instrument, and emanating out from an instrument all pose separate questions (and discrete constellations of intra-active agencies). There are notable differences between the acoustic profiles of various instruments, from instruments with strings vibrating in air (often with the aid of a resonant wooden box, e.g., cello); to struck instruments (either open, e.g., xylophone, or containing chambers or closed air passages, e.g., snare drum); to wind instruments, including key acoustic differences between those with one open end (e.g., clarinet) and two open ends (e.g., flute). The effect that sound waves' relationship to the entanglement of vibrating media has on the eventual sounding result mirrors the phenomena Barad describes. Sound waves in many wind instruments, for example, are dependent on their reflection or diffraction at key points. The famous acoustician Arthur Benade, for example, created an experimental clarinet in which the taper of the instrument and the tone holes were constructed so that the superposition of sound waves inside the instrument cancelled each other out. In this case, he took advantage of the diffractive phenomena present *within* the instrument to construct a clarinet that, although seemingly completely normal, would never emit a characteristic clarinet tone regardless of the virtuosity of the performer.

Benade's tongue-in-cheek tacet horn (named after a famous precursor to the modern clarinet, the basset horn) demonstrates the intra-active potential that lurks just beneath the surface of even conventional instruments. But the interior of the instrument is not the only factor involved. Acoustic studies of wind instrument players have shown that the body of the player has very appreciable effects on the sound waves produced, not only with respect to amplitude and frequency or ease of performing, but also as a resonating chamber that alters the acoustic profile of the instrument itself (cf. Li et al. 2015; Boutin et al. 2015; Hanna et al. 2018). Furthermore, in most wind instruments, the sound wave finishes outside of the instrument — that is, the final antinode of a sound wave touches the inside of the instrument, but the final node, which determines its frequency, is actually beyond the edge of the instrument. This means that perturbations to this area outside the instrument can have quite distinct effects on the sound waves the instruments produce (e.g., mutes on a brass instrument, some of which radically alter the pitch by disrupting the wave before its final node). It turns out that instruments, which exist in a layman's consciousness as sound-producing devices, are far more entangled in their surroundings than we musicians typically let on.

Many composers from the last century have sought to approach instruments naively, exploring their sonic potential as though ignorant of their traditional classical usage, and thereby exploiting their potential as acoustic devices to elicit new and provocative instrumental techniques. These pursuits ranged from Helmut Lachenmann's famous *musique concrète instrumentale,* in which he prescribed non-standard playing techniques to elicit new sounds from conventional instruments, to John Cage's indeterminate and chance-based arrangements of both musical and non-musical sounds and even entire instruments — which attitude Lachenmann, in turn, once derided as that of a "musical botanist" (Ryan and Lachenmann 1999, 21). These developments succeeded previous emancipations of non-conventional objects and sounds, from the Italian Futurists' celebration of noise to the early electronic music of Pierre Schaeffer, whose electronic *musique concrète* inspired Lachenmann's terminology, and Edgar Varèse, who considered music "organized sound" and "living matter" (Chou 1968, 19). The late twentieth and early twenty-first centuries have seen a remarkable proliferation of such engagements with instrumentalism and a full review of the literature on the use of conventional instruments to elicit experimentation in acoustics would not fit in these pages. They merely underline how agential realism can provide a potential avenue into instrumental experimentation that does not collapse as easily onto a binary spectrum spanning the fantasy of composition to the liberation of noise.

As an artist engaged in improvisation and composition alongside my career performing other people's music, I began to incorporate ideas from agential realism into my engagements with the instruments around me. In many ways, the most profound effects that this had on my working process was my conscious engagement with other agencies, especially the nonhuman. Experimenting with instrumental technique can quickly become curatorial, which is perhaps in part what inspired Lachenmann's contempt for the botanical. Discovering a new sound on an instrument can (d)evolve into an exercise in documenting it for posterity, not to mention the urge to showcase it as a kind of personal claim to its discovery or usage. Rather than searching actively for new sounds, I began to search for potential relationships, for agential proximities that could spark some sort of intra-action in one another. The pieces I produced in this period were often conceived as experiments of acquaintance, inviting instruments or other bodies into a proximity where their relation to one another would provoke acoustic results. Perhaps not all of them were equally successful, but they nevertheless proved extremely valuable to my own journey as I began to deepen my ability to provoke and learn from acoustic intra-activity.

The piece that accompanies this chapter is one of these experiments. Composed within the half year after my initial discovery of Barad's work, it was one of my first engagements with a piece that prioritized an empirical unfolding of agential relationships over a curation of the (desired) resultant sound. This piece, for alphorn with bassoon reed, was notated by overlaying a series of graphs with mathematical curves. Each curve was taken to represent one parameter of motion within the assemblage of mouth, bassoon reed, and alphorn mouthpiece. Additionally, the superposition of graphs allowed me to modify the way in which these parameters were read or processed by the performer (myself): instead of having each of the four lines describe a motion by itself, the demarcation of motion was instead the proximity of lines to one another. This means that a particular x–y coordinate for one parameter's graph would not always produce the same movement; rather, the actual motion would be dictated by its proximity to other curves. (Because the four graphs were on loose leaves of semi-transparent paper, these relationships would also change from performance to performance.) These various two- and three-dimensional motions of tongue, teeth, reed, and instrument highlighted the most obvious fault lines where these various agencies might abut one another. In hindsight, there is a curatorial superficiality to some

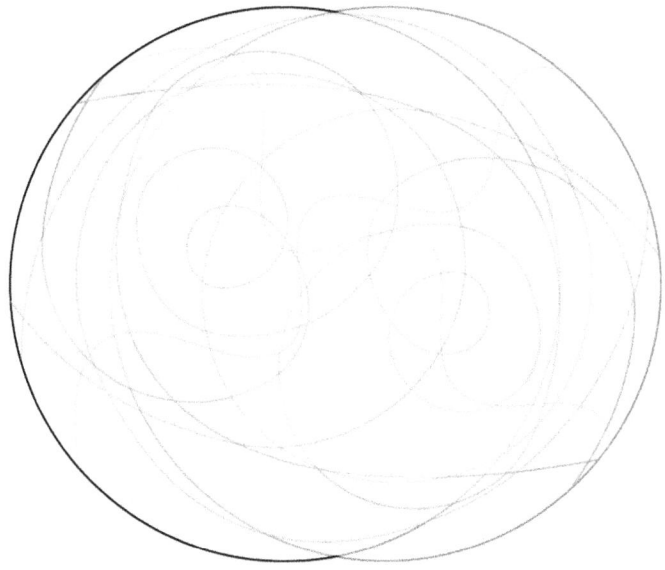

Fig. 3. Kevin Toksöz Fairbairn, *ay neden şeftali gibi kokuyor?* (2016), detail.

of the parameters I chose, but this particular constellation of agencies worked surprisingly well in that, while each of those motions alone has a quite predictable effect on the resultant sound, their superposition produced many unpredictable variations (fig. 3).

The performance history of the piece only underlines its vulnerability to particular constellations of agencies and environments. The premiere took place in the foothills of Vienna in the bitter cold. Not only did the weather conditions (and the four hour walk with an alphorn on my back) have a significant effect on the responses of the bassoon reed, my body, and the alphorn itself, but the piercing wind grabbed and threw the sound in all directions, producing unpredictable echoes and silences from neighboring hillsides.

As an attempt to explore the collision of agential forces and the intra-activity of sounding environments and their sounding visitors, the conditions could not have been more ideal! The second performance, preserved in the recording in this chapter, transpired under far more predictable conditions. In a beautiful, resonant concert hall at the other end of the very same 57A bus line in Vienna, I performed a short version of the composition alongside other works, although unbeknownst to me, a separate (but audible) harmonium performance began during the final minute of the piece. Even within the staid confines of a conservative Viennese concert hall, there was room for yet one more intra-active interpolation, an unpredictable confluence of agencies, congealed in that unrepeatable moment.

2

flotsam

> [L]et us not forget either that the feeling-itself-touching *of* the finger immediately is a feeling-itself-touch*ed of* the finger.
> —Derrida 2005, 163

Ever since childhood, I have always had an introverted, misanthropic streak. My interest in music stemmed largely from my ability to experience it alone, in time and space all my own. Although I grew up in a setting where school band was the primary introduction to music education, the weekly hours spent in said ensembles were the bitter pills I swallowed in order to continue my personal music experience. To this day, my favorite concerts are those I perform alone in a room, immersed alone in sound, hoarding all of the discovery and experimentation for myself, as though diluting the sound by allowing other bodies to soak it up would somehow diminish the experience. This predilection has always drawn me to evocations of the natural interiority of sound, searching for little keyholes that pass through the smallness of a concentrated sound to open up broader realms of sensation.

How does one find these interiorities, these keyholes of sound, while sitting alone in a room with a trombone? Trombone is a melodic instrument, designed to play one note at a time, unlike a guitar or a piano with extensive harmonic capacities. However, as a long metal tube with particular acoustic properties, a trombone does possess certain harmonic potential. The trombone is one of the least evolved instruments of the modern era. Although it has undergone some transformation over the past few centuries, it is roughly the same instrument that it was hundreds of years ago. This is because it relies on such a truly simple mechanism — a slide — that there has been no real need to develop. Other instruments have complex valves and keys and levers and whatnot, and while some string instruments also have relatively stable histories, even a piano, which relies on the rather basic action of a hammer striking a string, has undergone more technical evolution than a trombone. Nonetheless, despite its almost juvenile simplicity, the trombone has a lot to offer. It consists of a long, mostly straight tube with a flared bell on one end; in other words, it is little more than a glorified megaphone, intended to reinforce and amplify the natural tone and resonance of the tube. And that is the key part: as does any tube, a trombone has a natural resonance that results from the frequency of sound waves that correspond to the length of the tube. All that moving the slide accomplishes is lengthening the basic tube, thereby supplying a new set of sympathetic resonances.

If that were the end of the story, then a trombone would only play seven pitches. This is fortunately not the case, because the resonance of the tube reinforces a number of proportionally-related sound waves. A trombone in the key of B♭ resonates at the frequency of B♭ (roughly 58.27 Hz). However, many higher frequencies resonate within the same tube, in what amount to whole number ratios. These harmonic relationships, famously described by Pythagoras, occur at the same ratios as the harmonics on a string instrument, as well as in many other contexts. If the reader recalls the previous discussion of sound waves in a tube closed on one end, they will remember that the sound wave reaches an antinode at the end of the tube, with the node falling just outside the tube. Each higher harmonic on a trombone corresponds to the frequency of the next shortest sound wave with an antinode at the open end of the tube — in a trombone's case, at the bell; the mouthpiece end is closed off by the mouth and contains the first node. As mentioned, these work out to whole number ratios: the second harmonic is a frequency at a ratio of 2 to 1 of the first; the third harmonic is a ratio of 3 to 2; the fourth, a ratio of 4 to 3; and so on.

Trombonists learn to manipulate all of these pitches by adjusting a slew of bodily parameters such as air speed, size of the lip aperture, and more, allowing a full gamut of pitches and melodic potential. However, irrespective of buzzing lips and traditional trombone technique, these sympathetic resonances are an acoustic property of the tube itself. They inhere in the length of the tube, with or without the aid of the trombone player activating them. In fact, as one experiments more and more with the instrument, other means of eliciting these sympathetic resonances emerge. And so here is at least one answer to the question of what one might do alone in a room with such a tube, namely, the exploration of all manner of manipulations of the tube that provoke as many of these sympathetic resonances as possible. The rewards for exciting these sympathetic resonances can be quite dramatic, for as more and more of these harmonics are superposed on one another, the sympathetic vibrations become stronger and stronger, radiating outwards to other bodies. One can feel them in the flesh, in the bones, and as a performer, especially in the parts of the body in direct contact with the instrument. The piece that accompanies this chapter is the result of some of these experiments, and the harmonics I describe can be heard very clearly, especially from around the sixth minute onwards. It is a simple pleasure: sympathetic harmonies vibrating, resonating, resounding. As a singular person entangled with a tube and a certain amount of air, it is intensely rewarding to generate such a potent tactility, such a sensuous commingling of bodies in time and space. In these moments, sound truly becomes touch, and a single human alone in a room is just one body resonating among countless others in non-hierarchical, omnidirectional time and space.

Barad is similarly captivated by the tactile and sensual qualities of entanglement. She writes evocatively about the sense of touch that undergirds the entire science of physics:

> When two hands touch, there is a sensuality of the flesh, an exchange of warmth, a feeling of pressure, of presence, a proximity of otherness that brings the other nearly as close as oneself. Perhaps closer. And if the two hands belong to one person, might this not enliven an uncanny sense of the otherness of the self, a literal holding oneself at a distance in the sensation of contact, the greeting of the stranger within? So much happens in a touch: an infinity of others — other beings, other spaces, other times — are aroused. (Barad 2012, 1).

The specter of self-touch haunts her account of physics both classical and quantum. The gradual accumulation of scientific knowledge over centuries is, in some way, a glorious feat of ever-finer navel-gazing. There is a solipsistic drive to the progressive descent into the microscopic, down even to the quantum level, a unit so fundamental Barad calls it "a measure of the discreteness of nature" (Barad 2010, 246). And while much has been made of the weirdness and apparent illogicality of quantum physics, classical physics is, under closer scrutiny, hardly less counterintuitive. In Barad's reading, the hard science of physics is intrinsically connected to a basic, quotidian hapticity. Whether classical or quantum, physics encompasses the scientific pursuit of contact, the how and the why and the when and the wherefore. As a hard science, even the most experimental physics concerns basic questions about the tactile materialization of matter in the world. The study of laws of motion, of atomic interactions, etc., all reduce to some preoccupation with contact, either static or dynamic, a haptic thread running throughout. Barad writes:

> In an important sense, touch is the primary concern of physics. Its entire history can be understood as a struggle to ar-

ticulate what touch entails. How do particles sense one another? Through direct contact, an ether, action-at-a-distance forces, fields, the exchange of virtual particles? What does the exchange of energy entail? How is a change in motion effected? What is pressure? What is temperature? [...] What are the different kinds of forces that particles experience? How many kinds are there? What is the nature of measurement? (Barad 2012, 2)

Newtonian physics attempts to explicate precisely these concerns. Newton's laws of motion contend to describe the universe in astonishingly elegant simplicity: everything reduces to inertia, continuity, and balance. Followed to their natural end, though, these elegant laws lead to some rather curious conclusions. For example, touch itself, a fundamental element of the friction and equal-and-opposite forces that Newton describes, can only be understood as a sort of fraught attrition between particles:

A common explanation for the physics of touching is that one thing it does not involve is... well, touching. That is, there is no actual contact involved. You may think you are touching a coffee mug when you are about to raise it to your mouth, but your hand is not actually touching the mug. Sure, you can feel the smooth surface of the mug's exterior right where your fingers come into contact with it (or seem to), but what you are actually sensing, physicists tell us, is the electromagnetic repulsion between the electrons of the atoms that make up your fingers and those that make up the mug. (Electrons are tiny negatively charged particles that surround the nuclei of atoms, and having the same charges they repel one another, much like powerful little magnets. As you decrease the distance between them the repulsive force increases.) Try as you might, you cannot bring two electrons into direct contact with each other. (ibid., 3)

In this explanation, it turns out that the most essential aspect of touch is its absence. There is a certain poetry in that: the idea that deep in its most primal simplicity, our relationship to the objects around us is the precise inversion of our experience of it. There is an allure to the idea that all of the pleasure and pain that comes from physical contact can be reduced to an insurmountable repulsion, an unbridgeable gulf, a void. This mythology of the void pervades classical physics. The atom itself, the irreducible building block of matter, is supposed to consist almost wholly of void.

Physics does not end here, though, and as the global scientific navel-gazing apparatus became more and more capable of interrogating the atom and its constituent quantum particles directly, the understanding of this void radically changed. Rather than empty space with fixed particles orbiting a nucleus, the field of particles and charges that constitute the atom are instead more lively, both everywhere and nowhere. The electron's passage through the atomic void is not uncertain as has been popularly understood following Heisenberg, but indeterminate. Uncertainty implies an immeasurability, but indeterminacy implies a far more complex intra-active becoming, one in which this immeasurability derives not from a complexity of the system, but from its literal flickering of determinacy. In later chapters, I will discuss the relationship of indeterminacy and measurement more fully, but for this small issue of the unfillable void, I will constrain myself to remarking upon the shift that this requires in conceiving of space and time inside the atom. Barad writes:

> Heisenberg's uncertainty principle, once seen as the foundational principle of quantum physics, is at root an expression of the limits of human knowledge that result when a particle interacts with another in the processes of measurement. The uncertainty principle has now been replaced by the more fundamental notion of quantum entanglement, which is a contemporary expression of Bohr's 'indeterminacy principle.' According to the latter, measurements entail touch in the form of intra-actions, not interactions. (ibid., 12)

Particles interlace, threaded through each other's ongoing becoming in a flickering entanglement. The void that was presumed empty is in fact quivering with activity, with charge, with the interplay of particles. The repulsion that was understood to govern the enforcement of these necessary removes between particles is supplanted by a thick texture of intra-activity, of even single particles occupying space in and alongside themselves. The void, Barad tells us,

> is no longer vacuous. It is a living, breathing indeterminacy of non/being. The vacuum is a jubilant exploration of virtuality, where virtual particles — whose identifying characteristic is not rapidity (despite the common tale explaining that they are particles that go in and out of the vacuum faster than their existence can be detected) but, rather, indeterminacy — are having a field day performing experiments in being and time. (ibid., 4)

This indeterminacy is at the heart of intra-action, as discussed previously. A particle "collapses" or "resolves" into a particular subset of its fractal multiplicity through its entanglement with its context. The void is the indeterminate infinity of entangled touch. Each spatial or temporal crosscut of this entanglement constitutes the agential cut of Barad's intra-action, wherein a locally determinate subset of being emerges. Saturation, rather than emptiness, describes the void. The virtuality of this multiplicity is a constituent part of the fabric of the void, forming a crucial part of the (intra-)activity that unfolds uninterrupted. "[P]hysical particles are inseparable from the void, in particular they intra-act with the virtual particles of the void, and are thereby inseparable from it; the infinite plethora of alterities given by the play of quantum in/determinacies are constitutive inclusions in a radical un/doing of identity" (ibid., 6).

Barad's conception of touch emerges from the ceaseless, "murmuring" (ibid., 9) presence of infinite alterities in a constant dance of contact and non-contact. Intra-action details Barad's contention that existence is not a quality that something possesses, a static state of being, but rather a constant reenactment of entanglement, or in more simple words, contact, touch. What she calls the "un/doing of identity" is this continuous reenactment. Identity is never a "having" but is always a "doing." This "doing," though, is equally undone, as the intra-active embrace of particles and their virtual cousins shifts within a texture of in/determinacy. The consubstantiality of the indeterminate and the determinate in this unfolding highlights their hapticity.

It gets even more peculiar, though. Since the void is an interwoven web of entangled alterities, the precise nature of that alterity must also come under the (navel-gazing) microscope. Electrons emit and absorb photons in their in/determinate occupation of atomic time and space. Within and because of the interplay of these entangled emissions and absorptions, electrons intra-act not only with other particles and virtual alterities, but also with their own.

> [T]he electron not only exchanges a virtual photon with itself, it is possible for that virtual photon to enjoy other intra-actions with itself — for example, it can vanish, turning itself into a virtual electron and positron which subsequently annihilate each other before turning back into a virtual photon — before it is absorbed by the electron. And so on. (ibid., 5)

What bizarre form of touch is this? It is simultaneously identity-bending, self-immolating, self-consuming, self-producing. "Matter in its iterative materialization is a dynamic play of in/determinacy. Matter is never a settled matter. It is always already radically open" (ibid.). These particles are ajar to the fluid interplay of entangled identities, sifting through not only each other but also themselves. The coalescing of these particles into stable matter is not in spite of but because of this radical exchange and, one must add, intra-change. When Barad asserts that matter itself is a form of constant relating rather than a static state of being, she means it quite literally. The sea of contact that emerges from the void precludes their settling. The indeterminacy of instability is the foundation of matter's evolving determinacy and stability. Barad's 'in/determinacy' and 'in/stability' (ibid., 7) necessitate this atomic openness, a form of continuous, murmuring contact. "Closure cannot be secured when the conditions of im/possibilities and lived indeterminacies are integral, not supplementary, to what matter is" (ibid.).

Intra-action describes the agential cut whereby a localized entanglement of agencies collapses into a finite state. This finitude, though, is directly dependent on the steady circulation of these infinitudes, such that "every finite being is always already threaded through with an infinite alterity diffracted through being and time" (ibid.). This infinite alterity is the web of virtualities, in/determinacies, and in/stabilities that describe the intra-action of particles in time and space. Because this web emerges through the physical emission and absorption of particles, as well as through self-emission and -absorption as detailed, it entails very real contact. Unlike the counterintuitive suspension-by-repulsion of the aforementioned classical understanding of contact, a quantum understanding, for all its peculiarity, depends most fundamentally on a sense of physical touch. Barad writes that, "[i]n an important sense, in a breathtakingly intimate sense, touching, sensing, is what matter does" (ibid.). This morass of flickering in/stability percolates beneath a veil of finitude. "We may not notice the intimate relationships common to that level of existence, but, regardless of our blindness to them, they persist" (ibid., 8).

In addition to its radical vulnerability to the other, matter is also vulnerable to itself. Its dynamic openness weaves not only through the alterity of others, but equally through intra-action with itself. As "the self is dispersed/diffracted through time and being" (ibid., 6), it inevitably encounters its own dispersion. As a consequence, a critical strand of the intra-activity that rumbles through all matter is a radical, literal encounter with the self. "Hence, *self-touching is an encounter with the infinite alterity of the self. Matter is an enfolding, an involution, it cannot help touching itself, and in this self-touching it comes in contact with the infinite alterity that it is*" (ibid., 5–6, emphasis in original). The complexity of encounter precludes simple self-reflection, though. The in/determinacy of this self-encounter "is not reflection raised to some higher power. It is not a self-referential glance back at oneself" (Barad 2007, 88). It is instead a diffractive encounter, an entanglement not with a reflected or reproduced self, but with a genuine self-alterity. To reiterate the image with which Barad introduced the physics of touch, there is an exeriority within the interiority of the phenomenon, akin to the clasping of two hands from the same body. As Barad writes, "When two hands touch, there is a sensuality of the flesh [...] a proximity of otherness [...] the greeting of the stranger within [...] So much happens in a touch: an infinity of others — other beings, other spaces, other times — are aroused" (Barad 2012, 1).

Self-touch is an extremely evocative concept, particularly aesthetically. In the previous chapter, I explored some of the rudimentary ways in which an agential realist understanding of being in the world can inform a nonanthropocentrism in art. The spatiotemporal liberation of intra-action opens so many avenues of diffractive influence, and sound is a wonderful means to learn to listen to the nonhuman around us. Much more than just a chance to put one's ear to the ground and soak up the energy these agencies radiate, this means building a recognition of the ebb and flow of their tidal sweep through our own times and spaces and bodies, of learning to cultivate the ability to respond to their provocation. In simultaneous accord and contrast thereto, self-touch as physical entanglement is another window into this art of response-ability.

Barad's poetic ruminations on the inter-lacing of quantum and quotidian realities borrow so much from our sensory, sensual perception of the world, but she rarely draws from the vocabulary of sound and hearing. One of the only instances is in these reflections on touch, when she borrows the metaphor of "murmuring" from Avivah Gottlieb Zornberg, a biblical scholar who writes, "*the murmur is the message: the background hum of life — desolate, excessive, neither language nor silence — is what links us to one another*" (Zornberg 2009, xxi, emphasis in original). While Barad's language of touch revels in the perversity that matter exhibits, her evocation of sound taps into something more spiritual. For Barad, the flickering in/determinacy of self-touching particles is a vibrant, pulsating circulation, but as this coalesces into the deep murmuring in/stability of matter in its enactment, this vitality transforms into an OM-like hum. Much like this meditative syllable, Barad's sonic murmuring suggests an expansiveness of sensation, an openness to the touch of the world. The animation of entanglement takes on a reverberant quality, matter submersed in vibration.

In describing music performance, the composer Liza Lim once stated that "the musician *is* the first listener" (Lim in Rutherford-Johnson 2010, emphasis in original). It is an astute observation and a distinction rarely made, but as sound is produced by some assemblage of human, instrumental, and other agencies, the first human to experience the radiating vibrations of sound-become-music is the musician themself. They are not only an actor in this story, but also its first spectator. However, in the diffractive web of time and space, that web of superposed sound waves enacted by all of the media in a room, the musician is also the final listener. This is to say that, as the music diffracts through the full agential space, the reverberating sound waves circulate and return, saturated with the diffractive entanglement of other media in the room. The assemblage of bodies that initiated the sound are not only the first, but also the final, most peripheral agency to be subsumed back into this saturation.

Sound exemplifies this ubiquity of liminality. It has no matter of its own. There are no sonic equivalents to the protons and virtual protons that populate the atomic void. The crucial difference in the diffractive tapestry of sound and quantum particles is that sound is a massless phenomenon, an enactment and inhabitation of bodies entangled in space and time. Sound vibrations are woven into the tapestry of mattering bodies. The superposed diffraction of all of these agencies produces a coextensivity, each body bleeding into the next, and then receiving that same bleeding back in diffractive exchange. Any sense of impulse or centrality is circled back to within this web of touch, becoming a periphery, a borderland. Vibration enacts a ubiquity of omnidirectional touch, and then proceeds to continually re-enact it in resounding reverberation.

In the quantum scale, the term un/doing describes an interplay of self-dissolution, self-absorption, and self-touch. The redoing of self is always already implicated in its undoing. Sonic reverberation demonstrates a similar circulation of undoing and redoing, fused in a tidal rhythm of vibrating media diffracting waves through each other. Each touch of bodies is a simultaneous reflection and refraction, generating a whole new family of radiating agential ripples, so that a wave transmitted from one location is diffracted back to its source in a continual stream of redoings of the wave, each successively diffracted through other media along the way. Any impulse of a sound wave is already at the heart of its receipt. And because sound waves exist purely through the contact of mattering bodies, this means that any sonic touch is always already a self-touch.

One reason that the immersive experience of sound enmeshes so well within an agential realist framework is because it deconstructs linearity so comprehensively. Not only does it radiate and diffract in non-linear trajectories, but the manner in which it inhabits matter belies simple cause-and-effect relationships, opening it up to an agential realist account of in/determinate in/stabilities, that is, causes and effects entwined in their continual un/doing. An important ingredient in the spatiotemporal omnidirectionality of sound is this ubiquity of liminality — the way in which sound's haptic entanglement emerges from the subjective situatedness of bodies, each one both a locus and limit within its own perception. Sound's nonlinear saturation of diffraction circulates, but it does not circulate infinitely. Instead, waves circulate tidally, in ebbs and flows of mutual reinforcing, of amplification and interference. They may interact in sets, or migrate outwards to new peripheries. This un/doing recalls Kamau Brathwaite's notion of "tidalectics," which he proposed as a "rejection of the notion of dialectic," countering dialectic binarism with "the ripple and the two tide movement" (Brathwaite in Naylor 1999, 145). Similarly to diffraction, tidalectic thinking rejects binary oppositions and simple reflection.

Tidalectics summon the iterative quality of ocean currents, in which the singularity of individual waves is inextricable from their relationship to the entire current. The waves then breaking on a beach dissolves that singularity even more forcefully. The tide comes in and it also goes out, in global rhythms that span oceans. The linearity of concepts such as progress are dissolved in the tidalectic, for tidal motions are not simply transversal or even cyclical. They are not "characteristically circular or perpendicular or whatever other form one can construe in relation to space and time [...] [S]horelines come in different shapes and sizes just as tidal waves" (Nwadike 2020, 58). The tidalectic doesn't impose forms, but produces them emergently through the resistances and resonances of the world.

Sound waves vibrating in physical media participate in a tidalectic un/doing. The impulses of sound extinguish themselves as the friction and inertia of touch absorbs and swallows the sonic current. For its duration, though, that saturation of omnidirectional touch enacts the in/determinate tidal motion of waves that succeed and reinforce one another while diffracting through the whole. The tidal swell of touch, which carries a sound wave from its impulse out to some distant barrier and then back again, embodies a tidalectic polyphony, with diffractive currents intra-acting at all scales from the micro to the macro. A sea of touch, an oceanic current of interwoven vibrating air, flesh, wood, metal, and more: this is the murmuring vibration that supports the expansiveness of sound's presence in time and space. It never follows a simple, linear trajectory, but loses itself in eddies and swirls. The predictability of sound waves that we encounter in certain situations derives precisely from the tidalectic complexity of this dynamic in/determinate un/doing.

All of these things converge: the sense of touch that pervades the multitudinous un/doing in the atomic void; the murmuring sea of vibration and intra-activity that underlies this haptic in/stability; the tidalectic transmission of touch in reverberating sound waves. Self-touch emerges as a product of this murmuring, tidal motion, allowing the natural interference of superposition to enact a simultaneous dissolution and intimacy of self. In the piece that accompanies this chapter, *flotsam*, the gradual accrual of sympathetic resonances eventually overflows, producing greater and greater interferences before subsiding in simpler swells of fewer, more harmonically sympathetic vibrations. These reverberations are a tactile reminder of the performer's role as first and final listener, agentially both central and peripheral. The instrument and the air column inside it contain seething currents of resounding vibration; perhaps, after Barad, one can imagine it as a re/sounding tide of sonic hapticity. The sympathetic resonances that build up one on top of another vibrate inside the instrument, manipulated by the sympathetic superposition of slowly expanding layers of standing waves. As these waves swell to a breaking point late in the piece, enacting a tidalectic rhythm of recursion and retreat, the sheer physicality of the resonance transforms the performer, whose lungs continue to fuel this re/sounding assemblage, into a mere resonating body, just one more haptic spectator among many.

These resonances, layered tidally within the length of a trombone, demonstrate how sound enacts the intra-active potential of the matter it reverberates. These currents of vibration are only possible with sympathetic touch. Naturally, all media react differently to sound, with air or flesh or metal all responding uniquely to this haptic intimacy. The key factor that melts them together into a tidaletic unity is their response-ability, which is embodied quite literally by the ability of their matter to respond to stimulus. Sound operates on a macro level in a sea of media completely dissimilar to the quantum phenomena that Barad describes, and yet, just as her quantum microparticles vibrating in intra-active entanglement, sound waves also rely on the cyclical connecting fibers of touch. As Barad writes, "in a breathtakingly intimate sense, touching, sensing, is what matter does, or rather, what matter is: matter is condensations of response-ability" (Barad 2012, 7).

This intimacy allows the self-touch of these coalescing response-abilities to take on another dimension entirely. In explaining how "every finite being is always already threaded through with an infinite alterity" (ibid.), Barad references

Jacques Derrida's reflections on hapticity, as exemplified by his attempt "To Self-Touch You" (Derrida 2005, 265). Derrida conceives of identity as indebted to the other, stressing the receptiveness to difference that this requires. In citing his conception that self-touch "in no way reduce[s] the alterity of the other who comes to inhabit the self-touching" (Derrida 2005, 274), Barad affirms a particular tidalectic logic that emerges from the cyclical openness of intra-active self-touching. The self-touch of the other implies what is already clear, that "*self-touching is an encounter with the infinite alterity of the self. Matter is an enfolding, an involution, it cannot help touching itself, and in this self-touching it comes in contact with the infinite alterity that it is*" (Barad 2012, 5–6, emphasis in original). Infinite alterity enacts an in/stability, a seamless exchange within the un/doing of identity. The self-touch of the self and the self-touch of the other emerge from the same tidal relationships. As the haptic resonates, subsumed by the murmuring "*background hum of life*" (Zornberg 2009, xxi, emphasis in original), Barad echoes Derrida's subversion of identification in self-touching altogether: "there is the question of whether what is really at issue is not touching oneself per se but rather the possibility of touch touching itself" (Barad 2012, 5).

This is one of the only instances in which the sonic enters Barad's sensory vocabulary. In the murmuring hum of the universe, she finds the perfect expression of this concentration-cum-dissolution of identity. Barad is voicing a form of sonic logic, part and parcel of reverberation at its most fundamental. Touch touching itself describes the way in which sound inhabits matter as it radiates diffractively through its environment. Even as it resounds in and through the locus of its generation, it no longer exists as that generative agency. The self has dissolved and the vibration is just vibration: touch touching itself. If matter exists as a ceaseless un/doing, this metamorphic dissolution of being in intra-action becomes its most fundamental trait. Volatility exerts a force, it "torques the very nature of the relation between continuity and discontinuity to such a degree that the nature of change changes with each intra-action" (Barad 2010, 248).

Identity is dissolved into hapticity. Intra-active entanglement erodes the subjective self and its solipsistic sense of centrality. Instead, each agency is situated within this tide of mutual touching and being-touched, changing and being-changed: an infinite periphery with no center. Identity exists as an in/stability embedded in the fabric of reality, inhabiting a state of restless liminality. Similar to the way in which the omnidirectional democracy of sonic vibration is constrained and limited by the same hapticity that enables its generation and transmissibility, the indeterminate and unstable components of this quantum in/determinatacy and in/stability are necessary parts of the whole. For all of the fluidity that these systems demonstrate, they are anything but continuous. In fact, Barad reserves particularly withering disdain for the apotheotic role that classical physics reserves for the concept of continuity, the cornerstone of Newton's calculus:

> The presumed radical disjuncture between continuity and discontinuity is the gateway to Man's stewardship, giving him full knowability and control over nature. Calculus is revealed as the escape hatch through which Man can take flight from his own finitude. Man's reward: a God's eye view of the universe, the universal viewpoint, the escape from perspective, with all the rights and privileges accorded therein. [...] Matter is discrete, time is continuous. Place knows its place. Time too has its place. (Barad 2010, 249)

For Barad, there is no such mythical fixity. A continuity that defines itself in relation to discontinuity is similarly worthless when describing a non-binary, nonanthropocentric ontology. Such continuity can refer only to the obedient, deistic orbits of particles in a Newtonian world, but have no valence in the in/determinate, murmuring void that Barad evokes. The processes by which these quantum particles inhabit their space, themselves, and each other require an in/determinate reckoning of time and space. "The point is not merely that something is here-now and there-then without ever having been anywhere in between, it's that here-now, there-then have become unmoored — there's no given place or time for them to be" (ibid., 247–48). Intra-action is dynamic, and that sense exhibits a certain fluidity and liminality that traditional binaries cannot accommodate. These dynamisms include what Barad calls un/doing, in/determinacy, and in/stability, among others. The fluidity of entanglement, though, necessitates a similar dynamism of fluidity itself. The omnidirectional, omnitemporal intra-action of quantum entanglement entails an in/determinacy of continuity itself, which Barad calls dis/continuity. This is one of the most mystifying aspects of entanglement. It is already radical to assert that all being is relational rather than individual, that existence is a dynamic doing rather than a static possession, but this implies even further that that doing itself is subject to a relational, dynamic indeterminacy. Barad writes of the counterintuitiveness of dis/continuity:

> This strange quantum causality entails the disruption of discontinuity/continuity, a disruption so destabilising, so downright dizzying, that it is difficult to believe that it is that which makes for the stability of existence itself. Or rather, to put it a bit more precisely, if the indeterminate nature of existence by its nature teeters on the cusp of stability and instability, of possibility and impossibility, then the dynamic relationality between continuity and discontinuity is crucial to the open ended becoming of the world which resists acausality as much as determinism. (Barad 2010, 248)

The causal indeterminacy previously discussed entails a fundamental dis/continuity that upends even its own logic. Agential realism does not tear down one end of a binary formulation only to replace it with its inversion. It is not some glorification of discontinuity thrown in the face of Newton's continuity. It is a total embrace of a multi-dimensional liminality, entangling agencies in all directions of time and space. The continuous and the discontinuous are but one more spectrum dissolved into the murmuring hum of a relational, entangled ontology. Barad goes even further, citing the deconstructive lens which this dis/continuity applies even to itself:

> Quantum dis/continuity is the un/doing. (Even un/doing itself, as well as the notion of itself.) Even its appellation is at once redundant and contradictory: a smallest unit, a discontinuous bit... of discontinuity. 'Quantum', 'discontinuity' — each designation marking a disruption, bringing us up short, disrupting us, disrupting itself, stopping short before getting to the next one. [...] A passable impassability. (Barad 2010, 248).

The erraticism of these multi-dimensional concepts defines the iterative nature of intra-action. Entanglement demonstrates a sort of recursion, only it is a quantum version of in/determinate, un/stable, dis/continuous recursion. Because intra-action as a constant coming-into-being emerges from precisely this iterative quality, dis/continuity becomes a defining feature of any intra-active existing. "Being is not simply present, there to be found, already given. There is no fixed essence or substance simply there for the measuring [...] Mattering is about the (contingent and temporary) becoming-determinate (and becoming-indeterminate) of matter and meaning, without fixity, without closure" (ibid., 254).

Dis/continuity is a feature of non-hierarchized omnidirectionality similar to Manuel DeLanda's flat ontology, which describes an ontological realm "made exclusively of unique, singular individuals, differing in spatio-temporal scale but not in ontological status" (DeLanda 2002, 47). Only, in agential realism, that democracy of scale represents not singular individuals, which do not exist anyway, but are iteratively reconstituted through intra-action, but is extrapolated up to the qualities of un/doing that coalesce. If the intra-action of matter exhibits something akin to behavior, the ontological omnidirectionality describes that behavior rather than the resultant matter. Dis/

juncture and dis/continuity become forms of egalitarian indeterminacy, encompassing not only agents, not only space and time themselves, but scaling up even to the intra-activity that spans space, time and identity. Dis/juncture becomes a higher-order descriptor of acting and even thinking themselves, in tandem with the dynamism of emergent intra-action, more active than descriptive. The act of existing becomes "a way of thinking with and through dis/continuity — a dis/orienting experience of the dis/jointedness of time and space, entanglements of here and there, now and then, that is, a ghostly sense of dis/continuity" (Barad 2010, 240).

Like diffraction previously, dis/continuity becomes a powerful critical and philosophical tool. It torques scale, bridging higher- and lower-order interrelationships to build systems of "joins and disjoins," a simultaneous "cutting together/apart" (ibid., 244). In harnessing dis/continuity to think through sound, I began to call this dis/cord. It counters a binary spectrum of concord and discord with an omnidirectional, dis/continuous field. In fact, the words concord and discord stem from the Latin *cordus,* heart. Dis/cord is in fact a corporeality, a circulation of un/sympathetic vibration. Dis/cord is a resounding of interference, a multiscalar diffraction of diffraction itself.

I began this chapter by examining the phenomenon of sympathetic resonances. When they first appear in the accompanying recording, *flotsam,* they are ethereal, floating. They emerge from a murmuring hum, an enveloping wave sounding the fundamental of the instrument, the tube. The sympathetic overtones emerge from an actual manipulation of that sound wave. As I perform the piece, I produce this diffraction of waves by small manipulations at the end of the tube, not at the mouthpiece where I ostensibly generate the sound wave. Like a finger placed over the end of a hose, I am able to break the sound wave into streams of dis/cordant resonance. The intra-action emerges directly in the vibrating air column inside the instrument. Through the course of the piece, this dis/cordance intensifies. About halfway through, I also split the vibrations generated at the mouthpiece, contributing one further set of resonances to the entanglement — to continue my rather crude analogy, it is now as though there are fingers on *both* sides of the hose, a further dis/juncture all within the length of this simple tube. These manipulations at first produce the sympathetic resonances described at the opening of the chapter: simple Pythagorean ratios, easily discernible harmonic spectra, subjectively clear sympathetic resonances. The dis/cordance of *flotsam* emerges as these seemingly continuous resoundings accumulate. As a performer, I do not add any more layers of activity after the first half of the piece, but that activity itself intra-acts with itself. The dis/cordant reverberation of these activities and qualities of activities entangle, producing waves of affective interference. The intra-action of sympathetic resonance transforms over time from the meditative hum in the first minute into the dis/cordant columns of bellowing, shrieking dis/cordance in the fifteenth minute, before subsiding once more.

flotsam represents a progression within my own ability to work with an agential realist framework. As before, I sought to avoid fetishization of technical virtuosity on the instrument, discrete from creativity and executed in a strict chronological progression from composition to performance. I strove to find situations that already existed within the instrument itself, constellations of agency that would respond to some diffractive stimulus. This means experimenting with relationships, and with the interrelationships of those relationships. In many ways, despite the obvious mistranslations that can occur from the micro to the macro, sound's waveform and its incorporeality make it an ideal lens for diffracting an agential realist understanding of quantum phenomena into a scale more perceptible to humans. As Barad herself finds in examining the murmuring tapestry of touch that pervades existence, the resounding of sound itself can contribute to the discourse of agential realism. Sound emerges through the haptic entanglement of macro-particles, a resonance of multi-scalar diffractions. When we experiment with sound, this entanglement becomes forcefully palpable. Sound is touch, inhabiting our bodies; haptic entanglement surrounds and saturates the body, dissolving it into an omnidirectional fabric of reality where the non/borders of intra-active identity are un/done.

By following Barad, I developed my own understanding of sonic dis/cord. *flotsam* attempts to apply her understanding of dis/continuity at all levels, seeking theoretical and practical tools of dis/cord that can then elicit corporeally dis/cordant sonic phenomena. Experimenting with agential realism poses obvious problems to the world of music, which normally operates within a strictly directional spatiotemporal trajectory and seems to demand a great deal of agency from one primary source, the instrumentalist. Embracing the haptic agencies of instruments and the air inside them, of rooms and spaces and bodies, is a first step to dissolving this dependency on the linear and the hierarchical. Developing a sense of this haptic entanglement enables a more diffracted sonic awareness to emerge. Dis/cord becomes a way of thinking-with and thinking-through entanglement. It promotes a physical relationship that is liminal, omnidirectional, equally as agentially receptive as it is agentially generative. Dis/cord enables the "cutting together/apart" (ibid., 244) of bodies and their higher-order vibrations, allowing a dis/continuous practice to emerge intra-actively with, among, and from the world in its becoming.

When Barad describes matter as "condensations of response-ability" (Barad 2012, 7), she opens up a window into this sonorous realm. Agential realism describes the way in which matter iteratively becomes. This ceaseless hive of intra-action loses some of its peculiarity as one scales up from the quantum into the atomic, the molecular, and beyond. Sound in its dis/cordant cacophony helps show how this sea of in/determinate dis/continuity is woven into the tapestry of existence that we experience. Sound, as an immaterial and illusory presence, helps unlock the quotidian side of agential realism. The in/determinacy of reality becomes the tidalectic reverberation of matter, a dis/cordant resonance of liminal agencies all listening, echoing, resounding. Because these waves of sound saturate matter wherever matter comes to be, they amplify the very mundanity of the vivacious, sparkling, flickering web of intra-active quantum energy coursing through the universe.

3

jetsam

> That sound produced for me a version of myself entirely unknown to me until I was making it. As though the utterance itself was shaping me anew. That sound came to inform my whole sense of the relational world I had re-entered from another vantage point.
>
> —Singh 2018, 70

Many performers who are frequently on the road prefer to spend time alone in new concert spaces before performing. When the succession of trains, cities, and venues becomes a blur, it can be necessary to find a little time to inhabit a new space privately, to build a small intimacy there, however fleeting. Like many, I work hard to reserve some window of time in each new venue, in the hope that I can breathe deeply and make an acquaintanceship with the space while it is still just a room and not yet a concert hall. If I am lucky, I get some time when I first arrive, before any complications have had a chance to intervene. In these moments, I like to search for a spot near the border of the stage and the public; then I put my instrument together slowly, and before producing any other sound, I bring it up almost but not quite to my lips and blow a small stream of air directly into the tube from a few centimeters' distance.

This is by far one of my favorite sounds on a trombone. The full length of the instrument resonates, such that despite the delicacy of its near-inaudibility, there is a very deep resonance, a full-bodied breath en(coun)tering the acoustic space of the room. This breath allows the trombone to resound as an independent tube with its own acoustic qualities before I ever place my lips to it. This breath is also quite fragile, on the cusp of imperceptibility, thereby leaving space for the ambient sound of the room. These sounds — those from my breath, from the instrument, from the room — superpose for the first time. And although it is my breath that helps activate our first polyphonic assemblage, it is the least perceptible of them all. I get to enter the space primarily as a listener, implicated but peripheral, an exteriority-within-interiority. My first sonic memories of a new space are passive, vulnerable, open to inscription. It is my small attempt to invite the room and the instrument alongside me to make the first "marks on bodies" (Barad in Dolphijn and van der Tuin 2012, 52).

As things progress, I will eventually become more assertive in the space, both sonically and otherwise, but I try to capture something more communal in this first incisive intra-action, however superficial. This introductory sound I have described also happens to be the only sound that persists throughout the entire piece presented alongside this chapter, *jetsam,* which is an homage of sorts to this moment of acoustic acquaintance-ship. It is also a way for me to sneak this sound into a performance, either to remind me of that bubble of entanglement that existed before there was any audience present, or to seek that entanglement and its echoes while performing. *jetsam* helps me to remember that these moments are not isolated or stationary, but rather interlace themselves with other sounds and spaces and times. In thinking these sounds through agential realism, I take very seriously the fact that they, immaterial and ephemeral as they may be, still make very real marks on bodies. They intra-act in the world, and those intra-actions leave traces.

In the epigraph above, Julietta Singh writes about the traces that sound leaves on her body. In the book from which it is drawn, *No Archive Will Restore You* (Singh 2018), she attempts a reckoning of the various inscriptions retained in her "body archive" (ibid., 29). While recording inscriptions and marks left in or on her body from a variety of sources, Singh reserves special attention for her relationship to sound, which she terms "The Inarticulate Trace" (ibid., 51). More than anything else, she ties this corporeal "sound archive" (ibid., 76) to pain, its inarticulation stemming from "[t]hat space — physical, psychic, and temporal — from which you can no longer sustain a performance of yourself as a discrete and bounded entity [...] the body's breaking point, where you move from a recognizable version of yourself to something wholly estranging" (ibid., 58–59). Singh's concept of a sonic archive inscribed by extreme pain in the body evokes a strange relationship to temporality. Memories of pain can inscribe themselves indelibly in a person's body to the point that they can persist in a body part even after it has been separated from the body, but pain is also temporally bounded. Even when pain's traces are encoded or distributed throughout the nervous system or the rest of the body, it still stems from an initial processual unfolding. Singh's use of sound as a lens for demarcating pain accentuates this relationship, recalling the paradoxically immersive boundedness of sonic vibration.

For Singh, sound is an active substance. It is not a noun, with clear edges, but an enactment. Sound emerges as a form of viscous entanglement, an enacting of her ontology. In describing the polyphony of her own serious neurological pain with her newborn daughter's increasing vocal presence, she writes, "[e]very utterance she made hailed a kind of stunning promise of the future, the sounds of suturing herself to the world, while my sounds echoed a radical unraveling, the sound of unbecoming" (ibid., 73). Both of these acts, discovery and suffering, stitch together reality, not as a signification but as an enactment. They are gestural and gestative rather than fixed. So what would it mean for such a processual experience to be documented? How can it be reconciled to the idea of an archive? How would one explore its archival traces?

Singh is not the first to question whether documentation can preserve dynamic subjects. Suzanne Briet was asking already in 1951 whether living creatures or the light from stars could be archived, writing, "[i]s a star a document? Is a pebble rolled by a torrent a document? Is a living animal a document? No. But the photographs and the catalogues of stars, the stones in a museum of mineralogy, and the animals that are cataloged and shown in a zoo, are documents" (Briet 2006, 10). This didactically decisive conclusion revolves around not the quality of the document, but the quality of its use. Briet is already scaling up the idea of a document, defining it not by its physical characteristics but by the manner in which it can be embedded in human activity. Singh references the work of Erin Manning, who at the SenseLab in Montreal has developed the concept of an anarchive, which scales up this enactive interpretation of documentation even further. An anarchive pertains solely to the entangled web of actions and interactions that emerge from the generation or processing of archival material. It is related to archival material but is wholly enacted:

1. The anarchive is best defined [...] as a repertory of traces of collaborative research-creation events. The traces are not inert, but are carriers of potential. They are reactivatable, and their reactivation helps trigger a new event which continues the creative process from which they came, but in a new iteration.
2. Thus the anarchive is not documentation of a past activity. Rather, it is a feed-forward mechanism for lines of creative process, under continuing variation.
3. The anarchive needs documentation — the archive — from which to depart and through which to pass. It is an excess energy of the archive: a kind of supplement or surplus-value of the archive.
4. Its supplemental, excessive nature means that it is never contained in any particular archive or documentation element contained in an archive. It is never contained in an object. The anarchive is made of the formative movements going into and coming out of the archive, for which

> the objects contained in the archive serve as springboards. The anarchive as such is made of formative tendencies; compositional forces seeking a new taking-form; lures for further process. Archives are their waystations. (SenseLab n.d.)

Any body, human or nonhuman, could conceivably become archival material to be treated anarchivally. An anarchive is constituted by its iterative embedding in unfolding activity, an echo or resonance of intra-active entanglement. The traces that beings in the world enact upon each other do indeed create a form of archive, but the key quality of that archive is that there is no static materiality, only an iterative emergence, just as in the in/determinate un/doing of identity explored in the previous chapter. These bodies of knowledge are not objects abutted in space and time, but are intra-active components of knowledge-making as an empirical, generative process.

As previously discussed, agential realism reimagines identity as dynamic rather than static. This unfixed, emergent conception of identy is accompanied by a similarly dynamic understanding of sensory perception: even the objects perceived or the information learned are subsumed in a flow of in/determinate becoming. Anarchival thinking takes those emergent bodies and their progressive accretion of experience and embeds them in the same enactive gesture. The SenseLab speaks of an epistemic act that inheres entirely in the "movements going into and coming out of" the archival material that excites this motion (ibid.). This approach requires some level of entanglement, however implicit. It disposes of knowledge as a static container and unleashes it as an intra-active phenomenon realisable only in practice. Anarchivalism acknowledges archival material external to the anarchival act, suggesting that anarchival knowledge production ceases the moment it comes to rest, without the stimulus of the archive. Agential realism suggests that there may be no such moment when that movement comes to rest; the archival object is an illusion of stability within an uninterrupted, iterative flow of anarchival knowledge production.

In Baradian terms, anarchival thinking is an apparatus. Hailing from the world of physics, the language of agential realism is couched in the experimental terminology of hard science. In understanding the role that tools and the agents wielding them play in the world, Barad describes them as an apparatus. These apparatuses can be conceptual or physical, but like the anarchive, they are defined by their embedding within an emergent reality. This means that they are no less implicated in the coming-into-being of phenomena than the objects of their attention. They may be tools, but they are folded into the same fabric of reality as what they manipulate. And while they may retain pretensions of exteriority, couched in the language of observation, they are not separable from the phenomena they observe. As with the immateriality of the anarchive, apparatuses elude fixity, melting into the fluidity of the world they study. In short, apparatuses have no privileged status; they are neither more nor less entangled than any other intra-acting agency:

> Apparatuses are not inscription devices, scientific instruments set in place before the action happens, or machines that mediate the dialectic of resistance and accommodation. They are neither neutral probes of the natural world nor structures that deterministically impose some particular outcome [...] apparatuses are not mere static arrangements in the world, but rather apparatuses are dynamic (re)configurings of the world, specific agential practices/intra-actions/performances through which specific exclusionary boundaries are enacted. Apparatuses have no inherent 'outside' boundary. (Barad 2003, 816)

According to this understanding of apparatuses, it is possible to study the marks on bodies that existence accumulates, but not without leaving more marks on more bodies, including even the observing agent. Intra-action dissolves both centrality and externality. It embeds matter in an egalitarian liminality, distributed peripherally by the concomitant absences of either an inside focal point or an outside observation point (or critical distance).

The use of the body as an archive is inseparable from inhabiting a body. There is no neutral engagement, only entanglement. Observation is necessarily immersion. Apparatuses are "specific material reconfigurings of the world that do not merely emerge in time but iteratively reconfigure spacetimematter as part of the ongoing dynamism of becoming" (ibid. 2007, 142).

Apparatuses can come in many forms. For example, in describing her body, Singh outlines precisely the characteristics of such an embedded observational apparatus: "the ear […] the orifice that listens and stabilizes most acutely […] that sometimes selects what it allows in and at other times cannot help but to metabolize the noise that surrounds it" (Singh 2018, 105). In processing sound, our bodies exhibit the hallmarks of anarchival methodologies. They absorb the activity of sound, subject to the vagaries of vibrations diffracting through space. The choice is then how to engage, whether through a conscious attempt to listen, intervene, or ignore. That agency, though, can only come from a position that is already immersed. Any and all observation of sound is necessarily an anarchival act, a body slipping into an already moving stream. Singh describes this entanglement as metabolistic (ibid.), as though vibration effects a reconfiguration of the body as a form of nourishment, gestation, and circulation. Rather than archiving responses to stimuli, the body is instead enacting a form of anarchivalism. Inasmuch as the body is learning and growing in some way, this is anarchivalism as a form of research enacted through the entanglement of disparate agencies, or, as the SenseLab describes it, "a technique for making research-creation a process-making engine. Many products are produced, but they are not the product. They are the visible indexing of the process's repeated taking-effect: they embody its traces" (SenseLab n.d.).

This is especially true with respect to the sonic, because the bodies, i.e. the media in space, *are* the sound. They are what vibrates, what transmits, what diffracts. They are inscribed before, during, and as they continuously inscribe themselves. Metabolism is, in fact, not a metaphor. When Barad writes that apparatuses "iteratively reconfigure spacetimematter" (Barad

2007, 142), that is a literal description of any act of observation. Observation, in this case, listening, is an absorption and a metamorphosis. The ability a body has to selectively metabolize, as Singh suggests, is an expression of the agency of listening to reconfigure its environment. As anarchivalism suggests, there are no products. There are no objective/objectified instantiations at the end of listening, after the body has archived its sensual entanglement with sound. There is a "palpable indexing" (SenseLab n.d.) of these bodily traces, but they are in motion. The indices are already incorporated back into the system, they are already circulating, are already being digested.

Previous chapters have already explored how cause and effect are a nonlinear kneading together of agencies. In all of the entangled mess that sound turns out to be — intra-active and diffractive and messily ubiquitous — it is also extremely cyclical, or as I have previously called, tidalectic. These same cyclical qualities also create the metabolism that Singh describes. Sound exhausts itself in the frictive claustrophobia of matter. But it also excites other reverberations, other resoundings. A body that listens is always already responding. Listening is an embodied act, entangled in matter and in bodies, and as an apparatus of observation, it embodies the same response-able qualities that all matter does. The extent of that response depends on the agencies that coalesce around it, whether they amplify, augment, envelope, or truncate it. Any and all of those outcomes are already being digested as they occur, part of the metabolism of sound in matter. Because there is no non-vibrating matter, and therefore no truly silent or non-response-able matter, there is never any non-metabolizing void. A torporous metabolism is still an agential intra-action, and it is still recycling the anarchival indices of traces into new traces, however miniscule their ripples.

This does, however, open up the possibility of more dramatic responses. If they are not more animated, per se, they might still be appreciable in a wider, entangled context. If listening produces marks on bodies, and marks on bodies provoke intra-action i.e., anarchival metabolisms of response, then it is also possible that a sound excites more than just its own decay swallowed up by the inertia of the universe. It can excite more than just the reverberation of its own cyclical diffraction. Bodies react, and within the entropic entanglement of energies and vibrations that are already congealed in any given moment, there is always a chance that a sound will provoke more than just an equal and opposite response. The congealing of agencies that enact any moment are already digested and already digesting, meaning any listening metabolism might just spit out more than it previously swallowed.

This is part of the beauty of bringing the agential realist apparatus to bear on a macro scale. Sound may not be quite as bizarrely vivacious as the quantum world, but there are no atomic barriers at this level, either. The assemblage of agencies that coalesce in listening apparatuses can enact a far more global response-ability. The bodies that absorb these vibrations are already seething with stimuli, intra-acting across steep and distant spatiotemporal removes. This is what agential realist bodies do: they are never truly static, for they only exist as part of a ceaseless fabric of anarchival responding, remembering, resounding. Absorption is responding and responding is already absorption. Bodies' vibration in sound merely exposes this condition. Bodies are echo chambers, each mark, each trace a reverberating canyon, already resonating long before and long after any wave that might overflow it, producing the reaction that cascades outwards to other apparatuses listening, absorbing, and metabolizing.

Learning to compose and perform with agential realism has meant, more than anything else, learning to listen through agential realism. I know that I am always exerting agency and that there is no true form of passive, respectful listening-from-a-distance. When I try to perk up my ears and act the role of a dutiful, vulnerable listener, it is only an interpolation within an already ongoing, cyclical sonic metabolism. I have no illusions that consciously choosing to listen is substantively different than any other mode of engagement. As I cultivate my awareness of being superposed with other agencies, I attempt to engage myself as an anarchival apparatus, slipping into a stream of ongoing intra-action.

To describe this listening, let me first return to my pre-concert routine. I am in a room, near the edge of a stage, feeling the pressure of the air in the room on my skin and listening to a near-silence that reminds me of so many other near-silences that I have listened to before. I have brought along some vibrating perturbation inside me, a pulse, for example, that might already be faster or slower than it had been in one of those other, similar near-silences. The first jarring sounds to radically alter this sound are the percussive interjections of my instrument case and then my instrument. The sound of metal, bright and pointed, as I put together my trombone. I screw the slide onto the bell: a gentle, jangling metallic sound. Then I screw the bell flare onto the bell section and this one is a bit more unpredictable, some days it sounds like paper pages scraping each other, but on others, it shrieks like a seagull. Then there is the sound of its weight in my hands as I shift it into a playing position. This is not a sound I hear, just a pressure, a weight, an infinitesimal vibration — not a sound I hear, but nonetheless a sound I listen to.

At this point in my routine, I will pause, to recover again the near-silence. I like to think of this point as the beginning, the point at which the room and I properly make our acquaintance, although at this point our metabolisms are both already digesting, churning and absorbing. I pause and wait, listening to the sound of the pressure in my ears. When I feel that the near-silence has started to settle again, then I will begin, pursing my lips to make a small aperture, like the consonant *p* just after the air has puffed through the lips, and blow very softly into the opening of the instrument from just a few centimeters away. The bright, steady sound of the air entangles with the deeper resonance of the open tube, already complex even if nearly inaudible. An air sound like this is actually quite complex, sounding many overtones at once, almost percussive, and those resonances now distribute through the room. Unlike in the previous chapter, when the instrument is closed at one end, this time I am playing the trombone like a flute, lending it a totally different acoustic profile. It is open on both ends, and the sound waves stretch out in both directions, a standing wave, but with an antinode at each end of the tube. The sound waves stretch out to their natural nodal conclusion just beyond the confines of the instrument. This means that on the end near my face, the sound wave is reaching out towards my lips. Once again, I cannot sense this tactilely, but I listen to it anyway.

Agential realism provides a way to grasp this agency of listening. The dichotomy of acting versus observing is not useful, it is only confusing. It sets up false expectations of exteriority, either as an outside progenitor of new action or as an outside observer distinct from the subject of observation. Listening through agential realism explodes this simple binarism into a multi-dimensional field of interrelationships. Within this new topology, there is infinite variation of possible entanglements of acting and observing, of creating sound and of listening to it. As a performer, I feel a strong desire to keep the idea of listening constantly activated, but I also find it too problematic: the entire concept of listening as an extricable component of being and acting evaporates immediately upon closer inspection. Agential realism offers an alternative, a way to capture the meditative quality of intentional listening, while remaining firmly entangled in the intra-active fabric of the dynamic environment. When I listen in these moments, I am always a disturbance within the field. I am never a visitor, and all of the language of acquaintace-making is an intellectual tool to encourage an attitude of alertness, which prepares me for the response-ability that my agential entanglement in what I listen to demands.

In *jetsam,* this means listening not only to the steady stream of air that projects into, out of, through, and around this coming-together of instrument, space, and my body, but also to the sonic tendrils that stretch from this moment into other spatiotemporal topographies. As a form of self-consciously performed listening, *jetsam* does not devolve into a binary attempt to engage the space in dialogue. This delicate air sound that I have described at such excruciating length does not, in fact, generate the material of the piece, even though it persists, unrelenting, throughout the entire duration of the performance. Instead, it is the self-consciousness of my perturbation that takes over, that breaches the surface of foregrounded material. As I perform, this feels like nothing more than a topographical, perspectival shift. I am entangling myself in a new place within the entangled framework of what agencies had to come together to make this moment possible. The shrieking of my instrument as I assembled it turns into the bird-like cries that come increasingly to populate the sound world of *jetsam*. I allow my agencies to wander this topology, listening not only to the room but also to the detritus of my own awkward footsteps in the hall, my inarticulate shuffling and fumbling, and the imitations around me of those sounds that emerge from audiences or ventilation systems, or even, in one case, a dance class above the concert venue. These sounds also contaminate my assemblage with the instrument and its air stream. *jetsam* is an attempt to explore the counterintuitive coming-into-being that our entanglement both in- and out-side of space and time implies. And in the end, I have no doubt of my subjectivity and agency within this framework. The spiritual evocation of listening never shifts into some mythical sense of received wisdom, as though I am a vessel for sonic ruminations to pass through. Thinking intra-actively means subsuming oneself into the entangled agencies of the environment, while not being afraid to take ownership of the agencies one contributes. In a piece like *jetsam,* by seeking a fluid relationship between the provenance of sounds, I attempt to lose myself not in listening, but in the topographical exploration of my own role in creating this entangled mess of inter- and intra-vibrations.

In Barad's language, the enfolding of an observing apparatus into this multi-dimensional topology of agency is couched in terms of inclusion and exclusion. She writes of the impossibility of neutral engagement, pointing out that, given the infinite in/determinacy of intra-actions that swarm around each localized instantiation of being, every agency entangled therein is part of the machinery that makes some of these in/determinacies momentarily actual and others not. "*Apparatuses are the material conditions of possibility and impossibility of mattering,* they enact what matters and what is excluded from mattering" (Barad 2007, 148, emphasis in original). Matter exists as a constant un/doing of identities. Matter as a substance is an ongoing mattering and there are necessarily exclusions and inclusions at every step of the iterative process. The language of inclusion versus exclusion unfortunately reinforces a binary judgmentalism of positivity–inclusion versus negativity–exclusion. Despite that, if it is deployed in an agential realist sense, I still find the formulation fruitful for cultivating intra-active listening and performing practices, in large part because the discourse of aesthetics already follows the grain of an inclusive ideology in a very binary way.

Aesthetics concerns itself almost exclusively with ideas of inclusion. What is included in a piece of music? Which notes, and at which time? And who gets to decide? And who gets to alter or augment these decisions about inclusions? In the history of art and music, the answers to these questions lie in affirmations of specific claims to authorial authority. The logic of inclusion very quickly becomes linear and hierarchical. By contrast, an aesthetic of exclusion would listen to a piece of music and ask the questions, what notes are not in this piece? Which (non-)composers did not decide on these details? Who or what is not presently implicated in the performance of these specific notes? The infinite answers to these questions subvert the binarism of their formulation entirely and open the discussion up to a more multi-dimensional topology of awareness.

Anarchivalism couches the same concept in slightly different languages. SenseLab founder Erin Manning writes about Marcel Duchamp's concept of the infrathin: "A quality in the between, an interval that cannot quite be articulated" (Manning 2016, 3). Duchamp himself states that the qualities of the infrathin cannot really be described, but can only be grasped through examples. Manning, though, outlines a rough sketch of what exactly makes something infrathin or not:

> The infrathin cannot be generalized across experience: it is what makes experience singularly what it is, here, now. Between the event and the account of its retelling, an infrathin resides that will never quite be captured [...] the infrathin is a grasping at the singularity of an interval too thin to define as such and yet thick with the texture of lived relation. (ibid.)

Infrathin qualities can emerge from objects or experiences, from memories or actively-undertaken actions. What makes something infrathin is the coexistence of its appreciability and its ephemerality. It is passed over entirely while remaining utterly palpable. Manning also connects the infrathin to Alfred North Whitehead's formulation of negative prehension. Together with its inverse, positive prehension, negative prehension effects what is appreciable or not in our subjective, i.e., confined to ourselves as a subject, experience of the world. Negative prehension refers to what is somehow present but not felt, the infrathin thickness of "lived relation" that evaporates before it can be empirically grasped (ibid.). Agential realist inclusion and exclusion take this concept of prehension and torque it slightly, extrapolating an omnidirectional topology where the binary realities of inclusion/exclusion or positive/negative prehension entangle in an omnidirectional, gradated spectrum.

Listening is an apparatus of effecting and exploring this prehensive field. Listening as an active component of performing is a means of grasping the agencies of inclusion and exclusion that already necessarily inhere in the act. Bodies form an archive and the marks on those bodies form anarchives. These anarchives are the generative intra-actions that constitute the exploration of the vibrations that resonate at some infrathin moment in a performance, but they simultaneously explore the thickness of excluded vibrations, impulses, and sympathetic reverberations. Listening as an anarchival apparatus enables that-which-is-excluded to contaminate that-which-is-included in the ongoing mattering of sound. Anarchival thinking encourages one to see this as an active, agential process of knowledge production. When I listen, either in moments of lonely near-silence or in the midst of a concert, I am looking for ways to enable this contamination of excluded bodies, to wrest their physical entanglement from other constellations of mattering sound and re-inscribe them elsewhere and elsewhen.

An anarchival apparatus treats matter as a field of accessible contaminations. The non-centrality of this topology means that the full register of entangled anarchival indices are always in play. Even as some of these records come to matter and others don't, they are all embedded in the same prehensive web. Barad describes this contextual field of inclusions and exclusions as the "material-discursive" (Barad 2003, 810). They form a discourse not of language but of materialities. Their gradation of prehension, of coming to matter or not, is manipulated through a nonlinguistic but nonetheless discursive practice. An apparatus manipulates the material-discursive properties of matter. A listening apparatus can pivot and shift sound materially-discursively. Listening is an active difference-making agent in the world. As a form of observation, it makes inscriptions, but those inscriptions are not limited to the archival recording of experience. Rather, they pertain equally to the inscription of the anarchival production of knowledge in real time and space.

jetsam, for example, inscribes phenomena surrounding the spatiotemporal confines of the concert into the concert itself. By listening agentially across a broader swath of time and space, it creates a material-discursive vocabulary drawing from a broad cross-contamination of the concert-performing agents within their superposed empirical topologies. The piece becomes an inscription device, an archival form of listening that dissolves the archival object into a fluidly unfolding anarchival documentation. It embraces the delicacy of sounds that easily perforate one another, that are easily superposed. It takes the rich superposition of environmental sounds and forms an actively mattering inscription, encouraging an ebb and flow of inclusion and exclusion as some sounds come to matter and others do not. Emerging from the infrathin acts of attentive listening and inaudible near-silences, a practice of performative listening entangles itself directly in the texture of sonic materialization, embracing the inevitable entanglement of agencies in this material-discursive field.

Barad's invocation of the material-discursive is not only about the potential for discursive manipulation. The material-discursive properties of the observational apparatus are equally as embedded as the subjects of observation. This means that that apparatus is always on both sides of observation, on both sides of inscription. Barad writes:

> [A]pparatuses are specific material-discursive practices (they are not merely laboratory setups that embody human concepts and take measurements) [...] they are boundary-making practices that are formative of matter and meaning, productive of, and part of, the phenomena produced [...] apparatuses are themselves phenomena (constituted and dynamically reconstituted as part of the ongoing intra-activity of the world). (Barad 2007, 146)

In describing the apparatus, Barad indicates three stages of its entanglement with the world it observes: First, as a laboratory setup entering into the material-discursive realm of the world; second, as an agent actively forming both matter and meaning in that world; and third, as an object within that world being subjected to the same observation or material-discursive manipulation as it enacted itself. In other words, the apparatus joins the intra-active relationship, entangled in the inscribing of the world in an ongoing practice of anarchival knowledge production.

Apparatuses have bodies, and those bodies receive traces equally as they leave or record them. Returning to Singh's exploration of her own body as an archive, I am struck by a few entries in her index. In her account of the inarticulate traces inscribed by pain and joy and discovery and loss, she examines events throughout the course of her entire life. In her youth, she discovered the body's alienation from itself through pain. Each time her body crossed so-called thresholds of pains, she noted the sonic experience of these threshold-crossings. Whether verbal cries of distress or the physical sensation of vibrating, pulsating pain, these sonic records reverberate like sonic shock waves in her life, just as those left in the wake of an airplane accelerating beyond the speed of sound. In the course of her life, these sonic shock waves accumulate and resonate in her consciousness. But as she approaches the liminal edge of near-death, shortly after first giving birth, this alienation from the body through the reverberations of these sonic transgressions takes on a different form. Twice in this passage of confrontation with the edges of conscious existence, she marks new entries in her sound archive. First, while lying in the hospital following emergency surgery, she records the inscription made by screams of pain echoing throughout the long night, only, they are not her screams, but the screams of a patient in another room altogether, incisively entangling themselves in Singh's own experience of reality: "That woman, a patient I never met or saw but only heard, has stayed enduringly proximate to me. I can say with ease that I love her. She has grown into me and become over time a part of my body, an acoustic echo in my sound archive" (Singh 2018, 76). This other woman's shock waves of pain somehow supplanted Singh's own reality, effecting a cut — an exclusion and a respective inclusion within the mattering of the world. This record is followed quickly by the heartbreaking record of her father's journey to come to her in her crisis, to be by her side, a journey in which he ultimately died, not once but twice, an indescribable reverberation of pain and loss. Singh writes evocatively and descriptively of this "entirely imagined auditory event in [her] archive," his final exhalation, "a single gasping sound," an exclamation that sonically bridged the threshold of life and death: "That I never actually heard that sound makes it no less real to me, no less part of the compilation of materials, affects, and noises that make my embodied life what it is" (ibid., 79).

These observations on life and death, on thresholds and entanglements, sketch the way in which intra-active resonances weave themselves into dynamic spatiotemporal topologies. The roles of performer and listener are obscured beyond a simple consubstantiality. The apparatus that observes is deeply, indelibly inscribed itself, even as it records the inscriptions of others. Entanglement is not a metaphor for coexistence but a real inscription of marks on bodies.

When I perform *jetsam*, the implications of this inscription are deeply palpable. The inarticulate traces that this piece records on my body do not disappear. The piece emerges from a hazy veil of noisy air sounds, wriggling outwards into a room, seeking the threads of sonic agency that will enmesh themselves in myself and my instrument. *jetsam* begins with vulnerable sounds, incredibly open to the superpositional interference of other sound waves. As I seek to entangle myself in the hyper-awareness of this sonic moment, I also make my own body vulnerable, exposing my flesh to the unretractable inscription of the sounds that emerge through the course of the piece, slipping in from neighboring moments and slowly over-growing the *cantus firmus* of that initial, delicate air sound. I have spoken so much of the dissolution of identity in sound waves, through their omnidirectional democracy of intra- and inter-diffraction. But for all of its impersonality, the democracy of superposed sound waves is far from egalitarian. It is in fact ridiculously easy for one sound to dominate another. The trace of the softest sound will always be present, somewhere in the complex superposition of sound waves, but the sound waves with greater frequency and amplitude inscribe far deeper marks. These more assertive sound waves will reverberate longer and further, contaminating a wider environment of media traveling through walls, and leaving more physically tactile reverberations — the cloud of deafness that hovers in the aftermath of an explosion. Sound can inscribe truly deep marks on bodies: It can tear down walls and it can leave permanent deafness in its wake. *jetsam* is no exception. Despite the fragility of the sound that sketches its initial, nearly-silent locus of entanglement, it often unfolds into an eardrum-piercing shrieking. And just as the subtle air wave that stretched its antinodal fingers towards my body in the very beginning, this screeching also reaches and grabs and inscribes. *jetsam* tears into me, swirling together a sea of sounds that I love, but etching into me, at the same time, a pain that resounds permanently in my body, in my eardrums, and in the cavernous echoes of my memory. *jetsam* is the inarticulate scream of its own self-inscription. My body is an archive of the performances it has found itself entangled in. The traces and inscriptions left behind are my anarchival researches, intra-active phenomena that contaminate other entanglements in the course of my life at great spatial and temporal removes. *jetsam* is a practice of listening performatively, an inscription apparatus that opens me up to new spatiotemporal venues and allows me to take them with me, too, when I leave, entangled within the ineffaceable traces my body bears.

4

encyclical

> Pines also grow with fire. […] Some pines develop such thick bark and high crowns that everything can burn around them without giving them more than a scar. Other pines burn like matches — but have ways of ensuring that their seeds will be first to sprout on the burned earth. Some store seeds for years in cones that open only in fire: Those seeds will be first to hit the ashes.
>
> — Tsing 2015, 132

Both *flotsam* and *jetsam* are duos. I have only ever performed them by myself, though. When I first developed them, I did not perform them in public. Although they evolved out of intra-actions with variable environments, notably hotel rooms and concert venues on the road, they were, at first, purely private experiments. As I noted in the second chapter, such private concerts are actually one of my greatest pleasures. Throughout the years of their gestation, I had been thinking and reflecting about agential realism and continuing to read and reflect on Barad's work. Traveling became a form of metabolic digestion itself, affording me the time to read in long stretches, followed by a period of rehearsals and performances which would allow me to experiment in new spaces. In *flotsam* and *jetsam,* which were just two of the experiments from this period, I felt that the expansion from solo to duo helped me to capture an additional layer of entanglement. By recording versions of myself in one space and then performing a second along with that recording, I was introducing variables of space and time. Particularly in *flotsam,* because of the interference of resonances in clear harmonic patterns, the introduction of the second part intra-acted effectively with the first recording. Since certain resonances only emerged through their mutual superposition, the later version effectively mutated qualities of the first that were, in theory at least, immutably preserved by recording technology. This interpretation overcomes a basic superficiality because the sound waves of both recordings are sounding, superposing, and diffracting, all in real time and with appreciable consequences for the resonances.

At a certain point, when I felt that the pieces had grown enough, I began to also play them in public. This, though, was much more problematic. Although I had no compunction about performing alone alongside a pre-recorded, antecedent version of myself, I abhorred the idea of doing so in public. Performing alone in a room with a recording, I felt capable of embodying a response-ability, a capacity for relating between the two parts with a true sense of intra-action. I felt comfortable in the fact that, while performing the two parts together, the primary human attention in the room — mine — was always directed at the first, recorded version. As the sole human present and as an agential listener, my focus was firmly trained on the ghostly echo of my previous self's performance. Were I to perform this way publicly, though, this fine balance would be completely upended. As a live performer, my appearance as a soloist alongside an accompanying recording would upset the balance of intra-action that formed the core of my fascination with these pieces. Because of this, I have never been comfortable performing either piece publicly in this way, and have never done so. Instead, though, I had to find some other solution: a duo partner that could perform these pieces with me in real time, as intra-actively and response-ably as possible.

Eventually, I found the solution in another form of material engagement with sound, music, and instruments. Although I had not worked in the field for many years, I returned to my roots as an instrument builder. As a teenager, I apprenticed with a master brass instrument craftsman, and I have continued to work in this capacity off and on throughout my life, including designing and building all of my own instruments. When I build trombones or variations of trombones for myself, I often work on ideas over many years, making multiple attempts at a design before leaving it dormant for a while. I typically build something experimental, and then after trying it out, immediately deconstruct it again, saving the material for future experiments and further evolutions of my ideas. This lends a certain fluidity to the sense of identity of my instruments. Rather than having a single instrument that feels whole, I have a collection of them, sometimes with components that used to belong to each other. The entire assemblage of brass instrument equipment that I live with has a strange, entangled intra-relationship. As I worked with *flotsam* and *jetsam,* transitioning from a version performed alongside an ante-me to a new form of duo, I began to envision the latter as a duo of instruments rather than a duo of persons. I realized that, if I had misgivings about using the recorded ante-me in live performance, that did not preclude an ante-instrument from taking the stage alongside me.

I started experimenting with different pre-constructed pieces of trombones, finding ways for them to access the sound world of *flotsam* and *jetsam*. The full history of these experiments is not germane here; in any case, some of those experiments are simply other pieces now, and so belong to a different history. For *flotsam* and *jetsam,* I settled on a very particular setup. I collected a number of unfinished trombone bell flares, part-way through completion, meaning they had been spun into shape on a lathe but were not yet trimmed or brazed onto the instrument. I then mounted them on turntables, and, drawing from my extensive collection of the detritus of other instruments, built a series of metal attachments to play them as styluses in place of the turntable needle (fig. 4).

Fig. 4. Setup for *encyclical*.

Because both *flotsam* and *jetsam* have fairly static textures that evolve slowly over time, I was able to elicit many near-equivalent sounds from the revolving bell flare assemblage. The airy textures of *jetsam* were almost identical to the bell flare "played" by a very thin strand of metal just brushing the surface. With strands of increasing rigidity and girth, the more dynamic *jetsam* textures emerged, including the shrieking and screeching, which were nearly indistinguishable from sharp metal springs applied forcefully to the revolving bell flare. *flotsam* proved more difficult, and yet with a combination of similar provocations and the addition of a superball — apart from the turntable, the only part of the setup not derived from a pre- or de-constructed trombone — I was once again able to find sonic textures that made the new *flotsam* duo sound like the old.

However, the most interesting development in my relationship with this ante-trombone-cum-record-player unfolded separately from *flotsam* and *jetsam*. As I carried it around with me to practice rooms, hotel rooms, and concert halls, more and more frequently I began to let it run completely alone. In a new room, I would set it up first, turn it on, let some one or several bits of metal start sounding with the bell flare, and then go about other business. This could mean that it ran while I practiced trombone, and even now I still often leave the bell flare spinning and sounding while I warm up in the mornings. It could also mean simply sitting in a room and reading or resting or cleaning or cooking, with the revolving bell flare's song ongoing. And sometimes it meant simply listening, sitting down and giving the little concert my full, undivided attention. It is one of these concerts that is preserved in the accompanying recording, one of many iterations of this piece, *encyclical*.

In conjunction with the *flotsam* and *jetsam* concerts, these experiences prompted new interpretations of agential or performative listening. As I discussed in the previous chapter, I was already using agential realism as a means to devise new ways of listening while performing, but my experiences with the bell flare/turntable assemblage forced me to imagine even further variations on this theme. I was struck in particular by the strange role I played during the bell flare's solo concerts to one audience member. I was very much an agent implicated in the sound production: I prepared everything, started the turntable, made very conscious choices about which attachments to use, and decided the temporal durations and boundaries. However, those agential interpolations notwithstanding, I spent the bulk of my physical time engaging as a listener. It would be easy to analyze this situation along similar lines as those I used to address *jetsam* in chapter 3, that is, by viewing my role as an apparatus of observation entangled in the material-discursive intra-action by which some sounds, experiences, and bits of matter come into being and others are excluded. Instead, though, I found myself drawn to another corner of Barad's writings, centered around a particular experimental apparatus.

DIS/CORD

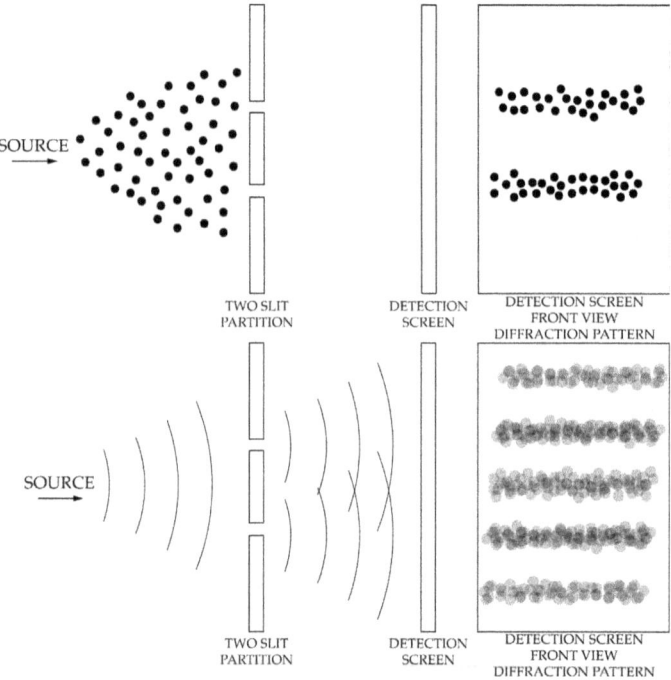

Fig. 5. Diffraction pattern comparison: particle versus wave. Illustration by the author (see also Barad 2007, 97–106).

Thomas Young first performed the two-slit experiment[1] in 1801, intending to test whether light was a wave or a particle. Although his work demonstrated that light was in fact a wave, or did enough to shift the understanding of it in that direction, debates and seemingly conflicting experimental discoveries

---

1   What I present here is an extremely brief and over-simplified account. For a more in-depth discussion, see pages 97–106 of Barad's *Meeting the Universe Halfway* (Barad 2007). There is also some variation in the literature as to the nomenclature of two-slit versus double-slit, which-slit versus which-path, etc. Given the preoccupation of the present work with the writings of Barad, I have followed her terminology throughout.

continued to raise questions, and doubt persisted as to whether both light and matter were truly waves or particles. Over a century later, the debate still percolated, and, as Barad writes:

> With the wave-versus-particle nature of light (and matter) at stake, yet again, it is perhaps not surprising that physicists turned to the two-slit experiment associated with Thomas Young. [...] From the perspective of classical mechanics, the two-slit experiment evidences a stark distinction between particle and wave behaviors. When particles are aimed at the partition with the double slits, we find that most of the particles land on the detection screen directly opposite each of the two openings in the partition [...] with a smaller number scattering off to either side. [...] When waves impinge on a barrier with two openings, they spread out as they emerge from each of the slits. The emerging waves interfere with one another (like the pattern one sees when watching two stones splash into a pond simultaneously). [...] This overall pattern exhibited by waves is called an interference or diffraction pattern. (Barad 2007, 100–101)

When this experiment was performed with electrons, which were ostensibly irreducible particles, they exhibited an interference pattern, indicating wave behavior (fig. 5). But when electrons were sent through the apparatus one by one, they exhibited particle behavior. And, even stranger, when multiple electrons were sent through one by one, temporally removed from each other, each single electron acted as a particle, but the total pattern indicated wave behavior. "Does an individual electron 'interfere' with itself? Does a single electron somehow go through both slits at once? How can this be?" (ibid., 102). Niels Bohr and Albert Einstein both famously developed thought experiments[2] based on this conundrum. In particular, they explored the question of how this behavior would change if the apparatus could

---

2 Much of the literature refers to these in Bohr's original terminology as Gedanken experiments.

actually determine which of the two slits the electron had passed through, i.e. to test the extent of entanglement of the apparatus of observation, as discussed in the previous chapter.

Amazingly, as technology evolved, it actually became possible to run Einstein's and Bohr's thought experiments in the laboratory, and effects such as the so-called quantum eraser could be empirically observed: by introducing a disturbance to observe which slit the light went through and so prompting it to travel through as a particle, the apparatus could remove the disturbance and the diffraction pattern would reappear, indicating that the light, which had already passed through the experimental apparatus as a particle, could somehow switch, and retroactively have instead passed through as a wave… in the past. It is quite difficult to adequately describe just how disorienting this is to those of us who grew up up thinking of time as linear:

> This result is nothing less than astonishing. What this experiment tells us is that whether or not an entity goes through the apparatus as a wave or a particle can be determined after it has already gone through the apparatus, that is, after it has already gone through as either a wave (through both slits at once) or a particle (through one slit or the other)! In other words, it is not merely that the past behaviour of some given entity has been changed, as it were, but that the entities' very identity has been changed! Its past identity, its ontology, is never fixed, it is always open to future reworkings! (Barad 2010, 260).

Although this experiment seems to show a quantum ability to alter the past, what Barad suggests is that the break in our understanding of the situation is more fundamental than that. Rather than exhibiting an exceptional aberration to the otherwise stable physical laws of the universe, she proposes that this reveals instead the mundane, non-exceptional, always-present indeterminacy that is actually at play in the universe at all times.

> It's not that (in erasing the information after the fact that) the experimenter changes a past that had already been present. Rather, the point is that the past was never simply there to begin with and the future is not simply what will unfold; the 'past' and the 'future' are iteratively reworked and enfolded. […] Space and time are phenomenal, that is, they are intra-actively produced in the making of phenomena; neither space nor time exist as determinate givens, as universals, outside of phenomena. (ibid., 260–61)

In building and listening to my instrumental assemblages and the raw metal spinning on turntables, I began to sense how these "phenomenal" characteristics of space and time could help me craft much more entangled ways of thinking through sound and its performance. To begin with, in contrast to a human body or a trombone or even a room, all of which exist in our imagination as holistic, bounded identities, the conglomeration of metal and turntables I had constructed presented on its surface as more of an assemblage. It looks and feels like an experimental apparatus. Once I began to use it to perform music, and especially once I would sit for hours listening to it passively, I began to reflect on both of our relationships as apparatuses in a Baradian sense. Although I participate by setting it up, once the assemblage begins to move, it generates sound independently of my intervention. Additionally by placing bell flares off-center on the turntable or by using bell flares with severe inconsistencies and "flaws," the resultant activity of the assemblage within its own domain would become quite unpredictable, outside of my control and capable of producing startling, unexpected changes over time. Consequently, I began to inhabit the role of listener more and more consciously, embracing the slow unfolding of sound as an enactment in, around, and on me as much as through my personal interpolation. Sitting in a room listening to these performances, I could think backwards through the temporal unfolding of this whole scenario and see my entanglement as a form of performative listening, rather than as a performance deeply inscribed by listening. This is largely just a shifting of the dial, a slow change of focus between a few lenses such that the entanglement of performing actions is skewed towards the teleology of listening rather than that of concertizing. It forced me to face questions about the superposition of my agency with that of the assemblage, though, especially as our entanglement revolved so fundamentally around the production of sound waves in real time and real space, tethered to certain moments and manners of performativity.

This fluid understanding of agential time and space was accompanied by a dynamism of the materials themselves. The assemblage was never fixed or finished. Building it was an ongoing practice, and I experimented continually with variations of the assemblage and its component parts. I was actively involved in constructing new versions constantly; instead of simply utilizing unused trombone detritus, that is its failed or trashed parts, I began to purposefully construct brand new trombone detritus expressly for the assemblage. What began as an experimental upcycling became a more concrete practice. As the project took on shape and ambition over time, the intimate relationship between the instrument-building process and the ensuing sounding result became more clear and more foregrounded. In fact, the instrument-building process was clearly as much or more entangled in the sound than even the process of preparing the assemblage and starting the turntable, although in the context of a performance, the latter action displays a more obvious agency in instigating sound waves in a specific space and time.

Through this complex entanglement encompassing instrument-building and performance, the two of us — the assemblage and myself — subjected each other to forms of the which-slit experiment. Within the multidimensional field of performative listening and acting, we were both capable of acting as listeners and actors. At one moment, for example, I may be active primarily as a listener, but the moment a particular seam of metal catches the assemblage and alters the sound, my intentional actions as an instrument-builder over the previous days would be suddenly implicated, warping my agential entanglement between its acting and listening dimensions. What had previously been an instrument-building action would be retroactively transformed into an act of listening. An inanimate assemblage would provoke complex webs of intra-activity with threads of agency stretching back through space and time in ever-shifting combinations. Our respective behaviors of listening and acting, instigating or reacting, were entirely contingent on the configuration of the performative apparatus. As with the wave or particle behavior measured by the two-slit experiment, the performances that I and this assemblage engaged in were capable of torquing not only the degree but also the kind of agency that we exhibited, all of which could shift in an instant with some variation in the sound or its setup.

This provided me one more avenue by which to reimagine the artistic process through agential realism. By enhancing and foregrounding the entanglement of agencies occurring beyond the boundaries of the nominal performance, I could more closely examine how these actions became retroactively activated or transformed as the physical sound waves were later triggered, diffracted, and expended. This working method entangled the creative process in all sorts of instrument-bulding activities: soldering, brazing, lathe-spinning, drilling, etc. These actions and tools were now part of the experimental/creative apparatus. They were part of the assemblage, even, since the particular variations in tool application were dictating the eventual behavior of the turntable, the bell flare, and every other aspect of the sound-producing assemblage. An awareness of the depth of this entanglement between instrument-building and sounding result also highlighted aspects of the performance's fragility. The sound world of *encyclical* is quite delicate, as the fragile resonances of the bell flare are activated and manipulated by tiny strands of metal bouncing and scraping on its surface. As my awareness of the relationship between my workshop and the performance heightened, this fragility of sound in turn contaminated the instrument building process itself. I could not help but be aware that, for example, the particular resonance of a bell flare could vary greatly depending on a single split second action I made on a lathe spinning at 3,000 revolutions per minute while slicing a piece of metal with a sharpened carbide tool. The fragile threads connecting all of these entangled agencies allowed me to explore even further agential realist implications for creativity. This creative process could expose and trace the intra-active entanglement of a much broader span of agencies over time and space. The assemblage of *encyclical* blossomed into an ecology, scaled upwards and entangling vast swathes of time and space within the delicate sonic world of an isolated, nonanthropocentric concert event.

These scales are reminiscent of the work of Anna Löwenhaupt Tsing, which bridges discussions of individual plants and plant species with explications of ecological-scale, "multispecies world-making" (Tsing 2015, 27). She pays particularly close attention to the way in which time and space bleed into one another through the complex interdependence of entire ecologies of agential beings. She describes these large-scale entanglements as "polyphonic assemblage[s]," rooted in the "patterns of unintentional coordination" that emerge from "the interplay of temporal rhythms and scales in the divergent lifeways that gather" (ibid., 28). This account resists the urge to exaggerate individualized or localized agencies, teleologies, and progressions. It would be easy to discuss these ecological entanglements through the lens of singular, butterfly effect events and their radiations of cause and effect, but this obscures the polyphonic superposition of countless such simultaneous butterfly effect moments. In describing these collaborative networks, Tsing invokes the idea of precarity. Precarity describes the fragility of individual moments, in which difference-making can still occur, but equally describes the large-scale interdependence of inter-generational intra-action between species and landscapes. For Tsing, precarity describes the fragility inherent in the seemingly monumental progressions of species, forests, and whole ecologies. It shifts attention away from linear narratives of progression and development and reveals the ateleological interdependencies that stretch in all directions of time and space. She writes that "[a] precarious world is a world without teleology. Indeterminacy, the unplanned nature of time, is frightening, but thinking through precarity makes it evident that indeterminacy also makes life possible" (ibid., 26).

The thread of indeterminacy as a generative phenomenon runs through the quantum entanglement of Barad to the ecological precarity of Tsing. Indeterminacy encompasses the nonlinear networks that constitute the world. When Barad uses it to counter simple, classical notions of causality, it reflects the fact that the entangled reality of the world is far too complex to fit into such simple, linear narratives. Similarly, Tsing's examinations of ecologies demonstrate how much the vitality of an ecosystem follows from the indeterminate precarity that binds everything together. Indeterminacy is a form of adaptive capacity. It reflects the fact that adaptation is a natural state and continuous function. Precarity highlights how adaptation is not a progressive evolution from stage to stage, but rather a superposition of many interwoven indeterminacies and interdependencies. Precarity, as an expression of indeterminacy, expresses how it is even possible that there can be "multispecies livability in the midst of disturbance" (Tsing 2017, 52).

In thinking concepts like adaptation and ecological balance through Tsing's idea of precarity, it becomes clear that these phenomena are not continuous in a classical sense. Although they continue unceasingly, their vulnerability to indeterminacy means that there is always a mixture of the discontinuous and the continuous. Adaptation is not linear, but encompasses the many overlapping contingencies of intra-acting organisms. Ecological balance emerges as much from disruption and extinction as it does from imperturbable continuity. Precarity describes a way of existing in the world not in spite of but because of these webs of indeterminacy. As Tsing writes, "What if […] precarity is the condition of our time — or, to put it another way, what if our time is ripe for sensing precarity? What if precarity, indeterminacy, and what we imagine as trivial are the center of the systematicity we seek?" (Tsing 2015, 26).

Tsing explores the implications of precarity by examining types of growth and adaptation that emerge in response to disturbance. She writes about situations in which disruption is not a crisis of progression, but rather exposes other, non-linear networks of polyphonic co-existence. She describes the assemblages of life and growth that exist in the shadow of linear progression:

> Without that driving beat, we might notice other temporal patterns. Each living thing remakes the world through seasonal pulses of growth, lifetime reproductive patterns, and geographies of expansion. Within a given species, too, there are multiple time-making projects, as organisms enlist each other and coordinate in making landscapes. (The regrowth of the cutover Cascades and Hiroshima's radioecology each show us multispecies time making.) (ibid.)

Regrowth becomes a theme. The cycles of indeterminacy that Tsing follows sometimes emerge especially or solely in the wake of disturbances that necessitate regrowth and reinvention. Tsing describes the regrowth of forests after fire: "After a forest fire, seedlings sprout in the ashes, and, with time, another forest may grow up in the burn. [...] The cross-species relations that make forests possible are renewed in the regrowing forest. Resurgence is the work of many organisms, negotiating across differences, to forge assemblages of multispecies livability in the midst of disturbance" (Tsing 2017, 52). She writes of how these disturbances enact new constellations of possibility and introduce new entanglements of ecological interdependency. Some species flourish in these settings, just as others fail. The epigraph to this chapter points out that even cataclysmic disturbances can trigger already-existing ecological networks that step into the breach: "Some [pines] store seeds for years in cones that open only in fire: Those seeds will be first to hit the ashes," (ibid., 132), and therefore, the first to flourish in the aftermath.

Disturbance and resurgence are fundamental parts of reality, part of the dis/continuous in/determinacy that Barad examines on a smaller scale, described in more detail in chapter 2. Agential realism is centered around the intra-active entanglements through which the indeterminate superposition of agencies "enact[s] what matters and what is excluded from mattering" (Barad 2007, 148). These same processes of iterative inclusion and exclusion are also borne out at the ecological scale that Tsing studies. Certain species can only exist in conjunction with others; other species can preclude the propagation of another. The processes of "multispecies time making" (Tsing 2015, 26) that Tsing relates outline how these complex entanglements emerge on many different scales and dimensions simultaneously. Decades-long interrelationships and momentary cataclysms are equally embedded in the precarious fusion of growth and resurgence.

Sound waves imitate Tsing's polyphonic ecologies. Like the species that emerge in particular iterations of resurgence, they are rooted to particular times and places. They represent specific material configurations in specific moments in time. Despite all of that, they are also deeply reliant on relationships of inclusion and exclusion that stretch across many scales of multi-agent time making. *encyclical* attempts to reveal these relationships. The impersonality of the performance, undertaken as it is by a nonhuman assemblage, sheds light on the disturbances, precarities, and indeterminacies that cohere in the coming-together of bodies that excite a sound wave. Sound requires the vibration of bodies and media not only to survive as an echoing resonance, but requires them also to materialize in the first place. Humans holding instruments and "making" music tend to occupy the imaginative, creative role in sound production, inevitably foregrounded by virtue of their apparently instantaneous control over what sounds are emitted or not. But this is the equivalent of assuming that a singular bee on a flower in a garden is responsible for the complex cross-pollinations and multispecies cooperations that produced that flower and its environment. By blending together elements of instantaneous sound production and off-stage instrument-building, *encyclical* highlights the creative and generative potential of entangled precarity.

Envisioning *encyclical* as one cross-section of an ecology also allows it to continue to grow. Describing this piece is more like describing a whole species than it is like describing a singular iteration thereof. With each new performance, whether public or private, and with each new trip to the workshop to produce new pieces, parts, and potentialities, the intra-active embodiment of *encyclical* grows. It is a performative practice, ongoing and iteratively dis/continuous. There is no linear progression of materiality linking each new iteration to the next; there is no established setup that evolves piece by piece, but rather a whole network of *encyclical*-ities that are variably interwoven and exchanged. Which sounds come to matter and which are excluded are an instantiation of precarity as systemic growth, as in Tsing's polyphonic ecologies. The sounds that form *encyclical* are only a momentary glimpse of singular bees on singular flowers, offering sketches of an ecological entanglement but not revealing the full network of relationships across time and space, which lead up to and out of this momentary glimpse.

But what does this say about the sound itself? As the instrument-building and performative listening all inscribe themselves more visibly in the process, how does this transform the actual sound waves that are excited in *encyclical*? What am I listening to all those hours on end, and how exactly does it relate to all of the lathes and drills and hammers that it has absorbed? The picture of these networks that I have just drawn is a problematic one: a singular moment that reveals the web of preceding and succeeding intra-active entanglements. Does the performative moment exist as a crucible, distilling these disparate indeterminacies into a potent materialization of actualized sound waves, vibrating palpably in fixed time and space? It presents an hourglass shape of entanglement whereby some agency sits at the center of the web absorbing the past and transforming it prismatically into the lived experience of the future. Perhaps the solipsism of our experience of the world predisposes us to think of the now-moments we experience as camera obscuras, filtering the past through the present and projecting it out the other side into the future. But reality doesn't break down on these simple linear spectra, and entanglement is not something enacted by a singular, enactive agency.

Instead of a linear progression in which continuous agencies are funneled into a present moment, sound's entanglement with its environment is far more reminiscent of Brathwaite's tidalectic rhythms, evoking waves breaking and receding, eroding and reshaping. The tidalectic is both collision and exchange, a network of traces that chart sound's simultaneously material and ephemeral presence in the now. Architect Bernard Tschumi writes of the "traces that time leaves on built form, the soiled remnants of everyday life, the inscriptions of man or of the elements — all, in fact, that *marks* a building" (Tschumi 1996, 77, emphasis in original). Tschumi is describing the entangled history of architecture, which is never a static structure and always an interpolation in a dynamic, tidalectic ecosystem. These buildings are also archives of marks on bodies, and anarchives of the traces and inscriptions that reverberate in material, recording histories of entanglement. Tschumi writes of buildings where the traces that remain are the erosions that eat away and obscure what once was. His traces are "the traces of decay" (ibid.), the holes and lacunae that time leaves within surfaces. These traces are powerful inscriptions, revealing how the absence of what has been eroded is sometimes a more potent trace than the legible record left behind.

By tracing the course of erosion in built form, Tschumi's formulation really only follows the eroded object left behind. It is a cascade, a multitude of precarities that progress only one direction. These traces succumb to a determinacy and a teleology despite their divergent multiplicity. But I want to know, what happened to the effaced crumbs of the eroded building? Are not their traces part of the record? I cannot help but feel that somehow these evaporated fragments have more to do with the sonic trace than the building left behind. The traces that time leaves behind are the eroded forms, but they are also and equally the compost accumulated by those erosions, washed outwards into other entanglements.

Tsing's descriptions of fire form an interesting counterpoint to Tschumi's traces. Rather than a documentation of decay and dispersal, these fires record the entangled cataclysms of disturbance and resurgence. How do we think through these fragmentations of forest, burnt remnants wafting away in the wind or washed into the ocean? These traces capture the interweaving of sound waves into their past and future entanglements. Fire is such a strange form of erosion and transformation. Like the buildings left behind by erosion, the remnants of flame are regarded with a strange sense of holism. It has always struck me as odd that, after cremation, the ashes that remain are conceived of as the remnants of the body. What of the huge proportion of the body that evaporated in the heat? Is that moisture less a fragment of what once was there? Do we leave ourselves blind to the trail of those traces simply because they resist casual observation? The evaporation and dispersal of traces in flame: This evokes the traces that sound follows, creates and leaves. These are immaterial materialities, already part of some other entanglement before their loss is even registered. The effervescent ephemeralism of the entangled destruction and resurgence of fires helps to map sound's tidal movement through material media. Each and every wave is an erosion, an evaporation, and an entanglement. These fragmentary sonic traces, vibrating and diffracting omnidimensionally, capture some hint of their entanglement. The idea that a sonic impulse inhabits a centrality of the moment is illusory, already a reverberation of an un/done identity that has passed on into other materialities.

Barad follows Niels Bohr in extrapolating one further insight from the entanglement of the apparatus with the object of its observation. As Barad writes, "Bohr's unique contribution is this: he proposes that we understand concepts to be specific material arrangements of experimental apparatuses. (For example, an apparatus with fixed parts is needed to make the notion of 'position' intelligible; whereas an apparatus with moveable parts is needed for 'momentum' to be intelligible)" (Barad 2010, 253). This follows from the indeterminacy of entanglement, that the fixity required for a concept to be determined requires some material coming-together of intra-active agencies, excluding some things from mattering and allowing others to come to be: namely, the concept itself. In proposing that concepts are in fact material configurations, Bohr has essentially proposed that they materialize as the evaporated traces of intra-active collisions.

At the heart of this evaporation is a dissolution. A seemingly holistic body or tree burns, and in the process the congealing of agencies and materials that constituted it are disentangled, unwound and released. One of the crucial differences between Bohr's concept of complementarity and Heisenberg's more famous uncertainty is that the latter refers to bodies, or particles, that are materially stable but uncertain with respect to measurement, while the former sees the indeterminacy as a literal, material matter. The making of determinacy entails an inclusive/exclusive unfolding of material intra-action. What is knowable is directly contingent on what is excluded from mattering, that is, "the contingent determination of meaning of any concept necessarily entails constitutive exclusions" (ibid.). The burning of a body enacts a new template of inclusion/exclusion on the intra-active entanglement of those particles, producing new and discrete subsets and entanglements of matter. Bohr's argument basically elaborates that the same process of material transformation is inherent in the congealing of a concept. This, in turn, depends on his observation that any sort of concept is a type of measurement. The entangled relationship of theoretical understanding with the material conditions it regards means that "*concepts are defined by the circumstances required for their measurement. That is, theoretical concepts* are not ideational in character; they *are specific physical arrangements*" (Barad 2007, 109, emphasis in original).

Concepts, then, are equally unstable and indeterminate. They exist in entanglement with that which they regard. This means that concepts are not a higher-order assessment of lower-order phenomena, but are phenomena of the same order as those which they theorize. While Heisenberg's uncertainty affords a concept the luxury to be uncertain but continuously valid, Bohr enfolds the concept into the dis/continuous entanglement through which material reality coalesces, congeals, disintegrates, adapts, and so on. "Concepts are indeterminate outside of the appropriate material conditions needed to make them intelligible" (Barad 2010, 253). The evaporation and disintegration of a burning body enacts new physical manifestations of concept. The subsumption of particles into new entangled relationships with air, earth, etc., is the enactment of new constitutive exclusions. When Barad writes that "[e]very concept is haunted by its mutually constituted other" (ibid.), she is describing the inarticulate traces that generate new materialities in time, re-constituting the dis/continous un/doing of bodily identity which, following Derrida, she calls a hauntology . Every body is always already, and has always already been, its other.

As previous chapters have reiterated, sound has no body of its own. It is a physical entanglement, a materialization of the interrelationship of proximity, but it exists in the diffractive transmission of energy rather than in the instantiation of its own material. But this account of Bohr's suggests that there is some body, some trace of sound, which emerges, precarious and resurgent, in the wake of its transmission. The observation of sound leaves the traces of its conceptual materiality. If it is listened to, if it is felt, if its waves touch any molecules, then its sounding reverberation has left these conceptual traces behind. In this way, it is the presence of sound that materializes rather than the sound wave itself. The traces that sound leaves on bodies inscribe its conceptual entanglement with the world. These conceptual traces of sounds are the intra-active, dis/cordant ephemera that emerge in the wake of the reverberant evaporation of sound waves. The tidal resurgence of sound deposits these concepts as shapes left in the eroded face of the world, as sedimentations of entanglement.

In *encyclical,* these conceptual sedimentations circle around the sound-producing assemblage. The act of listening performed by myself or any other audience reveals the conceptual exhalation of the sound, the evaporated traces of the piece re-entangling with other materialities as the sound waves radiate and subside. The instrument building that precedes and succeeds each performance is another form of listening. Instrument building entangles with the sound production of the instrument itself, absorbing the conceptual evaporations of sound and participating in their mutual "condensations of response-ability" (Barad 2012, 7). Because the instrument building remains responsive to the sounds that will later emerge, it encourages the entanglement of these activities. Over several years of slowly honing *encyclical*'s assemblage and my ability to respond to its sonic traces, I have allowed the instrument-building to drift into and out of the iterative materialization of the piece from performance to performance. The precarious balance of the two once again evokes the tides. They ebb and flow into each other's wake, non-linear and non-cyclical, but iterative, recursive, and entangled. The currents of the one can provoke the currents of the other, but the complexity of their exchange is as omnidirectional and unpredictable as the sea. It is precisely these tidal traces that form the materiality of the piece. *encyclical* manifests in its conceptual evaporation through the performance of listening and building-as-listening.

Fire and water: These elemental analogies describe the ineffable and ineffaceable traces of sound. The transformative, durational viscosity of fire and the tidal sweep of water both inform the precarity and resurgence of sound. It emerges through the commingled agencies of builders, listeners, and human as well as nonhuman performers, but these agencies slip away so quickly, resounding into silence as the sound waves themselves are expended in the inertia of their environment. It is only through their immersion in the accompaniment of the listening and the building that they then condense into these conceptual traces, these material sedimentations of metamorphosed intra-action. As in Tsing's resurgent forests, each fire fertilizes a new seed. As of today, I continue to build *encyclical* and I continue to listen, just as I will tomorrow. Although the piece has already grown over the years, augmented by additional turntables and bell flares, not to mention the accretion of public performances and audiences, it is always ever in some dis/continuous stage of regrowth — constructed, deconstructed, reconstructed; imagined, listened to, heard, reimagined. Each performance expenditure leaves behind a new set of traces, and the condensation of those evaporated traces are then part of the material fabric that nourishes and germinates the next phase of regrowth and resurgence. At this point, the piece is as much the building and the listening as it is the revolving bell flare and its metallic resonances. The conceptuality of the piece is its materialization, a sprawling ecosystem of entangled activities that are no longer possible to define or survey. That the piece continues — to be performed, to be built, to be listened to — is part of the rhythm of that system now, no longer contingent on the piece or its performance alone, but entangled with the vast network of traces that it has already left behind and ahead.

5

honewort

> Deafness is suspended above the blue tin roofs,
> And copper eaves; deafness
> Feeds on the birches, light posts, hospital roofs, bells;
> deafness rests in our men's chests.
>
> — Kaminsky 2019, 44

My body bears the traces of the sounds I have made. I have made them in concerts and I have made them alone in rooms. I have made them with instruments and with instruments making other instruments. I have absorbed them from the world and echoed them inside myself. I have uttered them in pain, when my body can no longer contain the surfeit of vibrations around me, uttering just one more overflowing cry in a sea of them. I have been obsessed with sound for decades and have lost myself so deeply in its sensuality that it has eroded and dulled my edges. I can no longer remember the first time I felt the inevitable repercussions of all this sound. Surely, at some point there was a first vacuous emptiness, like the sudden sonic void when my head is submerged in water. There must have been a first pealing tone before I came to recognize that ringing in my ears. These entangled moments have long since receded in the tidalectic flow of experience, but they mark me still, hovering on the cusp of every sound, the aural cobwebs floating in my peripheral hearing.

I come now to the pain of sound, because these are the traces that last longest. They mark the edges of absence before there is no longer even pain. For those of us that grow up hearing, we assume that sound is auditory perception, but the slow accrual of experience with deafness slowly teaches us that sound is vibration, that it has a materiality and a substance beyond our body or our perception of it. Ilya Kaminsky, the poet whose lines stand above this passage (and who is himself deaf), observes, "The deaf don't believe in silence. Silence is the invention of the hearing" (Armitstead 2019, n.p.). The hearing learn it, though, for as the sensory recedes, other entanglements seep in. The hearing invent silence to describe the absence of perception when they fail to apprehend the ongoing intra-active vibrations of existence. They use the word silence to demarcate the boundary of the known (the perceived). It imagines the edge of audible sound and invents its inversion on the other side of that border. Silence is a concept used to hold the fear of losing that perception; it is the outline of the shape of what we already know and hear. But there is no such silence, and the fear of losing hearing is embodied not in silence, but in noise. By some strange irony, the harbinger of hearing loss is just more hearing, an overloading and drowning of the senses: tinnitus.

Though I still hear quite a lot, I know ever more intimately the tactility of those sounds that leave their inscription in the language of tinnitus. Tinnitus is supposedly "the perception of sound in the absence of an external sound" (Levine and Oron 2015, 409). It is sound perceived in the body when there is no discernible stimulus outside it. This, truly, is a hauntology of sound: "the specter [that] cannot be fully present: it has no being in itself but marks a relation to what is no longer or not yet' (Hägglund 2008, 82). Tinnitus is the sound of the end of sound; it is perhaps the echo in the eardrum of the thousand million sounds inscribed by life, but it etches itself into perception as a sound all its own, a pronouncement of the peripheral extinction of hearing. Derrida, the progenitor of the hauntological "puncept" (Fisher 2015, 29) barely even mentions the term in the book in which he coins it,[1] demonstratively evoking the ephemeral liminality of hauntological substance:

> What is the effectivity or the presence of a specter, that is, of what seems to remain as ineffective, virtual, insubstantial as a simulacrum? [...] It would harbor within itself, but like circumscribed places or particular effects, eschatology and teleology themselves. It would comprehend them, but incomprehensibly. How to comprehend in fact the discourse of the end or the discourse about the end? Can the extremity of the extreme ever be comprehended? (Derrida 1994, 10)

So much of sound is an entanglement of antecedent agencies, but tinnitus embodies the hauntological echo of the eschatological. It is not an echo of sounds gone by, even if somehow those sounds summoned its spectral presence. It is an echo of absence, 'the extremity of the extreme.' Only, there is no outside of sound, not within matter, at any rate. Tinnitus is the spectral wandering of an end that cannot find an exit. It is the cosmic background image of the omnidirectional flat hauntology of sound, which permits no such silence.

In reading through Derrida's hauntology, Barad expands its scope to eliminate any metaphorical constraints of the spectral and reimagines it as the guise of intra-active entanglement. She introduces it first when discussing the 'quantum eraser' experiments, in which the two-slit experiment is manipulated to seemingly change the past. Barad's hauntology is the physical reality of "*phenomena* [as] *material entanglements enfolded and threaded through the spacetimemattering of the universe*" (Barad 2010, 261, emphasis in original). It is the spatial and temporal latticework that supersedes two-dimensional, linear spacetime. This is precisely why she takes issue with more classical analyses of this experiment that describe it as changing the past. As previously related, Barad points out that the past has not altered

---

[1] Derrida uses the term three times in the 221 pages of *Specters of Marx* (Derrida 1994).

because "the past was never simply there to begin with and the future is not simply what will unfold" (Barad 2010, 260). The entanglement of intra-active becoming means that the terminology of causation and succession cannot adequately describe the ontological intertwining of polyphonic temporal and spatial scales. She uses hauntology to distinguish this entanglement from a more classical ontology. In a hauntology, the echoes of past and future are not echoes at all, but active, resounding reverberations of the generative and the eschatological. The hauntological "does not signal a going back, an erasure of memory, a restoration of a present past. *Memory — the pattern of sedimented enfoldings of iterative intra-activity — is written into the fabric of the world.* The world 'holds' the memory of all traces; or rather, the world is its memory (enfolded materialisation)" (Barad 2010, 261, emphasis in original).

Barad speaks of the memory coextensive with the fabric of the world, and it is very easy to read something similar in the sedimentations of marks on my own body. This sedimentation of traces is a history of intra-actions, of vibrations, and of sonic coexistence. In the epigraph above, Kaminsky writes of a "[d]eafness [...] suspended" like a cloud, filtered out of the air and accumulated like pollen on "birches, light posts, hospital roofs, bells" (Kaminsky 2019, 44). Deafness seeps into our ears like particles into our lungs, as part of a rhizomatic, communal sedimentation. Much like the organic regrowth and resurgence of the previous chapter, this deafness tells of a different sort of cross-pollination and contamination. As the entanglement of the world in itself leaves traces behind, the erosion of bodies tells also these stories, of contamination and decay. The deafness I describe emerges from the hauntological specter of disembodied sound. Like all of the other processes in this book, it is a processual coming-into-being with and of the world, a knowledge-making practice of entanglement, but the threads that wind through this process deposit painful traces, exclude sensory identity, and produce knowledge of a materialized echo of the extreme. Deafness drips into us from the world, a precarious contamination of coexistence.

Although the piecemeal accumulation of countless sonic encounters has a lot to do with the ringing in my ears, I also have a pretty good idea of which specific sounds have done the most damage. Throughout this work, I have charted a slow course from onstage sound-making to its equal counterpart offstage, through an entanglement of listening, thinking, and instrument-building. The art and act of listening as a responseable performativity is the thread that ties all of these together. In thinking sound through a specifically agential realist framework, I have turned increasingly to the more liminal of these activities for my creative practice. As works like *encyclical* demonstrate, I have embraced actual, active listening as a genuine form of concertizing, and similarly, I have developed the craft of instrument-building as an intrinsic part of an ongoing creative practice (rather than as a form of tool-building, a pursuit in which the singular tool, once built, pays forward into other creativities).

This instrument-building, though, contributes more than its share to the oneiric history of my tinnitus, that echo of the unsounded. I cannot remember the very first moment I became aware of this spectral presence in my ears, but I do know when I became conscious of its increasing repetition. I can trace the lineage of my pain through specific acts of craftsmanship: machines with unexpected frequencies or sudden shrieks; moments of concentration perforated by unpredictable loud noises; sounds that simply pass through ear plugs as through air. One of the most damaging sounds I ever encountered was the use of a compressed air hose to clean moisture and metal chips out of small parts. Most of the time, it produced the sound of a simple air stream, but at certain moments, it would catch a shallow tube or an oblique surface just right, letting out a scream more piercing than almost anything else I've experienced. And yet it is part of a mundane task — cleaning — that is repeated over and over in the course of building. Its ubiquity and unpredictability make it difficult to protect against, and despite my best efforts, my body still bears the traces of innumerable such encounters.

This produces a rather curious situation. Although I approach instrument building as part of a carefully-developed practice of agential realist listening, I do so while wearing earplugs, shooting earmuffs, or even both. I seek to protect my ability to listen response-ably, but in doing so have no choice but to diminish my sonic awareness within the world. I cannot hear the resonance of the metal as I build it, although it would be audible at times, and although I would very much like to. Instead I am cast into a strange interiority, listening to the patterns of sonic and machinic vibrations not through my ears but through the rest of my body.[2] In fact, what I hear through my ears in these moments is only what has been conducted through my bones and my flesh, having entered my body through my torso or even the soles of my feet. What I hear are the resonances of my own body, capturing and echoing the reverberations of instrument-building.

Over time, though, I have come to love these sounds, as well. I know very intimately the soundfeel of each machine that I might use. Naturally, I can even diagnose problems with machines or interpret the behavior of the metal through this soundfeel. This new sense of sonic tactility takes on a prosthetic function as the exterior world becomes legible through a heightened interior sensibility. In this sense, Kaminsky's remark that silence is an invention of the hearing has never seemed more true. The loss of foregrounded aural listening enables the enskilment of a whole new order of embodied knowledge. I have built new sets of embodied tools and learned to navigate that space of instrument-building with a practice of heightened corporeal awareness. My sonic entanglement with the world has become a

---

[2] In moments of near-silence or inactivity it is possible to hear sounds from one's own body, such as heartbeats. These phenomena are widely known and discussed, especially with respect to anechoic chambers, which have even entered public consciousness. In my own experience, though, I have found the exterior sonorities that creep into this interior listening far more provocative, and they will remain the primary focus of the present work.

crucial component of my engagement with the materials I build with, welcoming them quite literally into my body and establishing a different sense of nonanthropocentric intimacy.

The development of this internalized soundfeel is far more than just a prosthetic augmentation of my craftsmanship, though. As much as I identify as a craftsman and enjoy the time I spend working with my hands, I am at heart still obsessed with sound. By spending more of my instrument-building time with ear protection (and with successively stronger ear protection), I have unearthed whole new sonic strata. And while I use this sensory capacity to augment my craftsmanship, far more often I am simply listening to it. I had never before focused on the sounds of my body filtered through and entangled with these machinic rhythms and timbres, and I loved it. Nowadays, I do not always have access to a workshop, and sometimes I go long periods of time without setting foot into these spaces or using these machines. When I return, these aesthetic entanglements in the workshop are what make me feel comfortable and welcome again. I find myself using machines with an air of conversation, greeting the space and its inhabitants and enjoying the familiarity of their company.

In the years since I began experimenting with agential realism, this embodied relationship to the instrument-building workshop has taken on a new dimension. I was already listening to the space, enjoying it tactilely, and developing familial relationships with some of the workshop's nonhuman agencies. At this point, though, I began to do so with a more conscious awareness of entanglement and nonanthropocentric agency. The machines are much stronger than I am (speaking in terms of pure horsepower), so there is always a sense of vulnerability in using them and in feeling their energy transmitted into my body. But the vulnerability that I cultivated at this point was more consciously response-able and also more overtly aesthetic. I was opening myself up to these sounds as forms of both coming-into-being and knowledge-production, an entanglement that Barad refers to early in her work as "[o]*nto-epistemology* — the study of practices of knowing in being" (Barad 2003,

829, emphasis in original). I started to see these experiences as more than just pleasurable byproducts of my ability to build; instead, they become consciously entangled acts of embodied research.

These reflections preceded and likely heavily influenced the trajectory of my work with the assemblages of *flotsam, jetsam,* and *encyclical,* but they also continued as a separate thread irrespective of those developments. In thinking sound through agential realism over a course of years, these ancillary activities became valuable laboratories for investigating all manner of phenomena, from the corporeality of sound itself to my body and its haptic entanglement with sonic materialism. I was not just building towards particular sound art projects (i.e., *encyclical* etc.), I was using my access to these experiences to learn about the nature of sonic intra-action and my agency within that network of interdependencies. Inevitably, this led to actual performance and recording apparatuses. I began to approach some of my favorite constellations of sound-production within workshops and record them through my body using contact microphones. This idea was inspired by a friend who wanted to listen to music, but who didn't trust noise-canceling headphones to offer the same level of protection as his normal ear protection. So, he kept his ear protection and bought a pair of bone-conduction headphones. I had never seen such a thing before, but was immediately entranced by this idea. Rather than using intra-corporeal conduction of sound to bring music into my body, though, I wanted to record the sounds of the workshop in my body and listen to them later as music. The piece that accompanies this chapter, *honewort,* documents one such engagement, a crosscut of the sonic environment in which I entangle myself.

Agential realism had ushered me through a whole range of sonic engagement. I had variably experimented with a broad range of experimental setups, from performing onstage while cultivating relational intra-action, to performing through an entanglement of acting and listening, to exploring the onstage potential of performative listening through offstage creative work, to now harnessing offstage creative work to produce onstage works. These many strands of agential realist experimentation were overlaid, diffracting through one another. None were continuous, so the ebb and flow shifting from one project to another through their polyphonic intermingling leant them a sense of interdependence. Even while performing one of these pieces, I will find myself referring to another, whether overtly in the sound or through the conceptual configuration of the experience. *honewort* has a special place in this corpus. Often, being on stage is the most vulnerable that I feel as a performer, but because *honewort* grew out of an engagement with pain and decay, it combined that onstage vulnerability with a concentrated engagement with offstage vulnerability, that is, with the painful traces of sound recorded in my response-able body.

There would be no *honewort* if the pain and vulnerability did not persist. The ongoing fragility reminds me repeatedly that this is part of what it means to be response-able. The openness to being affected by the other is the risk that the traces it leaves will hurt. The erosion of the body can lead to intra-activity, but it can also foreclose intra-activity. There are radical indeterminacies and exclusions that are enacted by pain and loss. They isolate. The dissolution of the self can sometimes be a radical evaporation embracing a dis/continuous flood of new entanglements, but at other times, it only heightens the sense of solipsism and frays the threads that connect one to the world. The disembodiment of tinnitus contributes to this alienation; it emanates from the ear itself.[3] It registers as a complexly external sound but exists internally. It confuses and distracts, and by hovering on the periphery of the body, intensifies the feeling that a binary separation from the outside exists. While wearing ear protection can soften the vulnerability to new perforations of the self, it cannot stop the tinnitus itself. Tinnitus simply exists, like a

---

[3] I refer here to my own tinnitus. Not all forms are related to ear damage; there are also neurological forms that emerge through other material-discursive entanglements.

parasite — other but self — a contamination of binarism infecting the solipsistic isolation of pain.

This descent into the self can be dangerous. In an agential realist account, there is no such thing as a separable self. There is no stasis, and within the dynamic unfolding of existence, we are not singular, bounded entities. Entanglement extends to all micro and macro scales, from the quantum to the molecular to the full body holobiont and even beyond. But lived experience does not always make this easy to discern, and pain is one of the most efficient agents at breaking down the scaffolding of those entangled interrelationships. The intra-active nature of reality does not depend on our conscious experience of it, but as I hope I have demonstrated in previous chapters, the cultivation of response-ability can enable the perception of these wider-ranging entanglements to emerge. However, when Tinnitus erects a barrier along the edge of one's senses, the isolated sense of self that it constructs only accentuates the locus of pain. This damage to the body can inhibit an agential realist awareness, capable of recognizing that the self is not a locus of any kind. It can obstruct the ability to engage with the world while accepting that the self is neither a centrality nor a hub; even the mind is distributed, entangled, a Zeno's paradox of localized identity.

Although Barad deals primarily with the phenomena of the micro world, she still questions basic notions of self-identity, subverting easy formulations of individuality and its necessarily binary division of self versus other. In one instance, already previously cited, she describes the tactile experience of clasping one's own hands together: "[M]ight this not enliven an uncanny sense of the otherness of the self, a literal holding oneself at a distance in the sensation of contact, the greeting of the stranger within?" (Barad 2012, 1). She unfolds this into the exegesis on self-touch and haptic entanglement addressed in chapter 2. This self-touch resonates with the sonic rabbit hole that I experienced while working with ear protection, in that by descending into the self, I found traces of the reverberant other. Barad's understanding of the ephemeral in/determinacy of quantum entanglement is quite similar. No matter how tightly wound the self or the identity may become, still, "[a]ll touching entails an infinite alterity. […] Even the smallest bits of matter are an unfathomable multitude" (Barad 2012, 7). Not only is matter not merely entangled with other intra-active agencies, but because its identity is also fragmented dis/continuously in space and time, it is entangled with itself. It contains an infinite alterity, and coexists with entanglements of itself. Not only is the concept of the individual dissolved, but the binary of self/other is equally so.

This diffraction of the self in space and time makes the self also part of the other. As Barad writes, "Each 'individual' always already includes all possible intra-actions with 'itself' through all the virtual others, including those that are noncontemporaneous with 'itself'" (Barad 2012, 7). The infinite alterity that inheres in the self is a diffraction of both self and other, a non-contemporaneous noncoincidence of identities. This superposition of selves and others is an extremely key component of the world Barad maps. The intra-action of matter entails a vulnerability, which necessitates some element of response-ability. In examining the noncoincidence of the self, this response-ability becomes a response-ability to the other and the self, to the infinite alterities that thread through these entangled un/doings of identity. Barad sees this superposition as a crucial and inevitable scaling up of the epistemological and ontological implications of agential realism.

> Entanglements are not a name for the interconnectedness of all being as one, but rather specific material relations of the ongoing differentiating of the world. Entanglements are relations of obligation — being bound to the other — enfolded traces of othering. Othering, the constitution of an 'Other', entails an indebtedness to the 'Other', who is irreducibly and materially bound to, threaded through, the 'self' — a diffraction/dispersion of identity. 'Otherness' is an entangled relation of difference (*différance*). Ethicality entails noncoincidence with oneself. (Barad 2010, 265, emphasis in original)

This extrapolation of obligation from response-ability can be contentious. For Barad, it follows accordingly from the implications of agential realism. She cites the trajectory of ethics in philosophy from Levinas to Derrida, noting the crucial role that the presence of the other plays. But Barad's other is different from theirs. It is not a materialization that one faces, and certainly not a reflection or opposition of the self. Unlike her predecessors', Barad's vulnerability to the other is not only exterior, but opens up also to the infinite alterity of interior entanglement.

> The sense of exposure to the other is crucial and so is the binding obligation that is our vulnerability, our openness. […] But what would it mean to acknowledge that responsibility extends to the insensible as well as the sensible, and that we are always already opened up to the other from the 'inside' as well as the 'outside'? How might we come in contact with or least touch upon an ethics that is alive to the virtual? This would seem to require, at the very least, being in touch with the infinite in/determinacy at the heart of matter, the abundance of nothingness, the infinitude of the void and its in/determinate murmurings. (Barad 2012, 9)

This ethical dimension opens outwards from the collapse inwards of the self. Ethical obligations or responsibilities to the other are not formulaic; they do not follow from simple relations of proximity. "[E]thics cannot be about responding to the other as if the other is the radical outside to the self. Ethics is not a geometrical calculation; 'others' are never very far from 'us'; 'they' and 'we' are co-constituted and entangled through the very cuts 'we' help to enact" (Barad 2007, 179–80). Intra-action deconstructs simple geometrical formulations of causality and identity. These same dissolutions affect also this ethical dimension. In many ways, the ethical obligation that Barad purports is tied most closely to its entanglement with these two other concepts: identity and causality. She dissolves identity in the pluralistic entanglement of intra-active coming-into-being and she subverts causality by enfolding it into the intra-active development of living-as-knowledge-making practices. Both are subsumed into the dynamism of agential realism, discarding any residual conceptual baggage from stasis or singularity. The ethical dimension is similarly dissolved and entangled, becoming a part of the coexistent web of ontology and epistemology: her ethico-onto-epistemology. This chimerical neologism does not indulge in casual conflation, but rather expresses the very crucial constraints that agential realism reveals in the world. Being, knowledge, and coexistence are emergent phenomena, dynamic and vibrant in their iterative unfolding in the world and entangled through their shared intra-active genesis.

In other words, the ontological, epistemological, and ethical facets of our existences are not merely superposed but rather consubstantial. They are made of the same fabric. Agential realism suggests that we have an obligation to engage with "the world of which we are a part, not because it is an arbitrary construction of our choosing but because reality is sedimented out of particular practices that we have a role in shaping and through which we are shaped" (Barad 2007, 390). If our ontologies are entangled through the bizarre un/doing of in/determinate identity in agential realism, then our ethical relationship to the world is not one of merely choice or non-choice. It exists entirely outside that binary opposition because it is entangled in the same web of emergent becoming from which we derive our epistemological understanding of our placement within it. In dissolving the notion of the other, the entanglement of ethico-onto-epistemology also dissolves the notion that vulnerability is inherently othered, absorbing it into the iterative dynamism of intra-action.

> The point is that more is at stake than 'the results'; intra-actions reconfigure both what will be and what will be possible — they change the very possibilities for change and the nature of change. Learning how to intra-act responsibly as part of the world means understanding that 'we' are not the only active beings. (Barad 2007, 391)

The entanglement of ethico-onto-epistemology directly affects the "possibilities for change" in the world. The vulnerability to the other is an active component of intra-action. This is where agential realism differs somewhat from other flat ontologies. The implications of agential realist entanglement are not egalitarian at all, as one of the most fundamental characteristics of intra-actions are that "they enact what matters and what is excluded from mattering" (Barad 2007, 148). There are necessarily exclusions, and those exclusions will accumulate, as will the inclusions that constitute what becomes part of the ongoing materialization of reality. Agential realism completely undermines traditional notions of singular, unilateral agency, but it also opens the individual up to higher-order networks of agency that constitute the vulnerability and openness inherent in ethico-onto-epistemology.

The neologism response-ability encapsulates this topology of non-singular agency and its vulnerability to the inclusive/exclusive dimensions of agential realism. It contains elements of both responsivity and responsibility, but is also critically different. Both responsivity and responsibility carry strong overtones of obligation, the absence of choice. The former has an almost biological imperative: response follows stimulus. The latter is a form of commitment: to be responsible implies that the foregoing of that responsibility is an abdication. Response-ability, though, entails something much more flexible. It implies a vulnerability not only to stimulus, but to the fact that not all stimuli are equal. It is an obligation of sorts, to maintain a flexibility that can accommodate both the expected and the unexpected, but it does not imply that *all* potential responses are obligatorily manifested. Response-ability follows from responsibility and responsivity, but incorporates those concepts into a broader network of dynamism, in which the non-flat aspects of the world's unfolding are part of the stimuli, part of the web of response. Response-ability exists in an omnidirectional field of influence in stark contrast to the binary formulations of responsivity (stimulus/response) and responsibility (independence/obligation). It outlines a way to cultivate ethical responses in the context of nonlinear relationships of self and other, cause and effect, and before and after.

As I have repeatedly noted with respect to sound, the dynamic and non-singular aspects of intra-action do not completely displace the natural imbalance of agencies. Barad's insistence on the ethical component of her triumvirate follows from her acknowledgment of intra-action's lived ramifications in the world. These effect literal marks on bodies, they change reality and, as Barad makes clear, affect equally the very reality of change itself (what becomes possible and what is foreclosed from possibility). Sound reifies this starkly: first, the very fundamental differences between vibrating media shows that not all substances are equally able to respond, or equally open to the interpolation of new sonic vibrations; and secondly, certain sound waves have radically different capacities for enabling or foreclosing other sonic intra-actions — which is to say, certain sound waves inscribe more dramatic traces on other agencies' bodies. It is not enough just to say that viewing sound through an agential realist lens reveals the underlying entanglement of bodies and agencies, encouraging us to tap into those tapestries of spatiotemporal intermingling. Such logic would still imply a vulnerability of visitation and a separability from the phenomena and their repercussions. Barad warns us that an accurate account of the subsumption of the self into the entangled intra-activity of the world demands not only a cultivation of response-ability, but also an acknowledgment of the uneven agential topologies that result therefrom.

This is more than just an ethics, it is a veritably tidaletic reverberation of vulnerability. Agential realism engages not only with the superposed presences of selves or others, but with the accumulated echoes and resonances that they generate. These ripples diffract, too, as the web of superposed agential reverberation vibrates through the world — the 'murmuring' tide of being that Barad describes. Resonances propagate but also expire, swallowed by the interference of other bodies and other resonances. A reverberation of vulnerability is a reverberation of alterities, opened up to one another and commingled in a vast superposition of mutual amplifications and interferences. The language of sound is perfectly suited to conjure up this type of entanglement. Sound — immaterial materiality, the unending exchange of energy and vibration — makes manifest the deep intra-active fluidity of the matter it excites. It echoes at every level of matter, from atoms to black holes, but never in precisely the same way, always diffracting new patterns of interrelated matter. This radical fusion of inevitability and variability fits perfectly into Barad's /-language, the punctuation of dynamism. A reverberation of vulnerability can exist only through in/determinacy and dis/continuity. Barad coined such neologisms to evoke the swirling, non-binary, superposed topologies of supposed antonyms like determinacy and indeterminacy, continuity and discontinuity. The dis/continuous is neither simply continuous nor simply discontinuous; the emergence of each unique momentary fusion of these two concepts is effected intra-actively. The constant flow of exclusions and inclusions of mattering reflect the very real discontinuity that is at the heart of each continuity, and vice versa. They are not poles on a spectrum, but are entangled resonances of each other, radiating from each inta-action and always already diffracted through the next intra-actions. The vulnerability of each agential cutting apart/together is a crucial facet of agential realism, and the foundation of a Baradian sense of response-ability.

As I lived and thought through these concepts personally and artistically, I found this dis/continuity seeping out of all my sonic work. The inversions and reversions of performative listening and acting are dis/continuous; the entanglement of apparatuses in the sounds they make and observe are dis/continuous; the blossoming of sounds from instrument-building and of instrument-building from sound are dis/continuous. In working with sound and agential realism, the dis/cord that I have produced comes ever closer to amplifying this dis/continuity, bringing the pulse of in/determinacy ever nearer to the surface of sound. I wrote before of dis/cord as a corporeality, a circulation of un/sympathetic vibration, a resounding of interference, a multiscalar diffraction of diffraction itself. As a concept it stands for the omnidirectional enactment of sounding in/determinacy, in which the vulnerability of sound in bodies is subjected to the ateleological subsumption of opposites. The coexistence of pain and pleasure in sound are two such dis/cordant poles. *honewort* relates the corporeal history of pain inscribed in the body by sound, of the body's responsive collapse into solipsism, and of sound's response-able contamination of that same body through other, ever more corporeal channels of dis/continuity and dis/cord. It records a reverberation of bodies that produce sound by producing themselves, that intra-act neither purposefully nor aimlessly. *honewort* is the documentation of a response-able intra-action, of my body bearing its accumulated traces into new intra-actions, and experiencing the dis/cordant soundings that it can still inscribe upon the world, and be inscribed by.

Dis/cord comprises the corporeal response to vibration. It embodies the entangled nature of intra-action and participates in the resonance of those entanglements in space and time, tidally and omnidirectionally if not equally or uninterrupted. The unique patterns that these intra-actions excite are the fabric of reality, the resounding of intra-active coming-into-being. They change the nature of change and inscribe indelible traces on our bodies before receding again. As an artistic practice, dis/cord has allowed me to open up my relationship to sound and other sounding bodies. A practice of response-able sounding is not about some mythical holism of nonanthropocentric resonance, although it enables the emergence of such resonances. It is, instead, a way of developing new relational practices, ongoing entanglements of coming-into-being that allow for the excitation of sounds not yet predicted. The story of the pieces included here, which chart the course of my journey with agential realism, is that the practices themselves don't just assist in the curation of sounds, but actively generate them. The rich entanglement of bodies is only the beginning of dis/cord, which reverberates through time and space, activating new bodies while yet diffracting through its sources, dis/continuous and in/determinately creative.

Bibliography

Armitstead, Claire. 2019. "'I will never hear my father's voice': Ilya Kaminsky on Deafness and Escaping the Soviet Union." *The Guardian,* July 19. https://www.theguardian.com/books/2019/jul/19/ilya-kaminsky-interview.

Barad, Karen. 2003. "Posthumanist Performativity: Towards an Understanding of How Matter Comes to Matter." *Signs: Journal of Women in Culture and Society* 28, no. 3: 801–31. DOI: 10.1086/345321.

———. 2007. *Meeting the Universe Halfway.* Durham: Duke University Press.

———. 2010. "Quantum Entanglements and Hauntological Relations of Inheritance: Dis/Continuities, SpaceTime Enfoldings, and Justice-to-Come." *Derrida Today* 3, no. 2: 240–68. https://www.jstor.org/stable/48616359.

———. 2015. "On Touching — The Inhuman That Therefore I Am (v1.1)." Preprint ms. https://www.academia.edu/7375696/On_Touching_-_The_Inhuman_That_Therefore_I_Am_v1.1_.

Benade, Arthur. 1973. *Trumpet Acoustics.* https://ccrma.stanford.edu/marl/Benade/documents/Benade-Trumpet-1973.pdf.

Boutin, Henri, Neville Fletcher, John Smith, and Joe Wolfe. 2015. "Relationships between Pressure, Flow, Lip Motion, and Upstream and Downstream Impedances for the

Trombone." *Journal of the Acoustical Society of America* 137: 1195–209. DOI: 10.1121/1.4908236.

Briet, Suzanne. 1951. *What Is Documentation*. Translated by Ronald E. Day, Laurent Martinet, and Hermina G.B. Anghelescu. Lanham: Scarecrow Press, 1951.

Chou, Wen-Chung. 1968–69. "East and West, Old and New." *Asian Music* 1, no. 1 (Winter): 19–22. DOI: 10.2307/834006.

Cobussen, Marcel, and Nanette Nielsen. 2017. *Music and Ethics*. London: Routledge.

Cox, Christoph. 2018. *Sonic Flux: Sound, Art, and Metaphysics*. Chicago: The University of Chicago Press.

Cusick, Suzanne. 2013. "An Acoustemology of Detention in the 'Global War on Terror.'" In *Music, Sound and the Reconfiguration of Public and Private Space*, edited by Georgina Born, 275–91. New York: Cambridge University Press.

Derrida, Jacques. 1994. *Specters of Marx*. Translated by Peggy Kamuff. New York City: Routledge.

———. 2005. *On Touching—Jean-Luc Nancy*. Translated by Christine Irizarry. Stanford: Stanford University Press.

Díez-Fischer, Santiago. 2015. *sensitive switch*. Self-published.

Dolphijn, Rick, and Iris van der Tuin. 2012. *New Materialism: Interviews and Cartographies*. Ann Arbor: Open Humanities Press.

Evens, Aden. 2005. *Sound Ideas: Music, Machines, and Experience*. Minneapolis: University of Minnesota Press.

Fisher, Mark. 2015. *Ghosts of My Life: Writings on Depression, Hauntology, and Lost Futures*. Winchester: Zero Books.

Hägglund, Martin. 2008. *Radical Atheism: Derrida and the Time of Life*. Stanford: Stanford University Press.

Hanna, Noel, John Smith, and Joe Wolfe. 2018. "How the Acoustic Resonances of the Subglottal Tract Affect the Impedance Spectrum Measured through the Lips." *Journal of the Acoustical Society of America* 143: 2639–650. DOI: 10.1121/1.5033330.

Haraway, Donna. 1992. "The Promises of Monsters: A Regenerative Politics for Inappropriate/d Others." In *Cultural Studies,* edited by Lawrence Grossberg, Cory Nelson, and Paula Treichler, 295–337. New York: Routledge.

James, Robin. 2019. *The Sonic Episteme: Acoustic Resonance, Neoliberalism, and Biopolitics.* Durham: Duke University Press.

Kaminsky, Ilya. 2018. "from Deaf Republic." *The Massachusetts Review* 59, no. 1 (Winter): 37–44. https://www.massreview.org/sites/default/files/06_59.1Kaminsky.pdf.

LaBelle, Brandon. 2010. *Sound as Hinge.* Berlin: Transmediale. https://www.brandonlabelle.net/texts/LaBelle_SoundasHinge(2010).pdf.

Levine, Robert A., and Yahov Oron. 2015. "Tinnitus." In *Handbook of Clinical Neurology,* Vol. 129: *The Human Auditory System: Fundamental Organization and Clinical Disorders,* edited by Michael J. Aminoff, François Boller, and Dick F. Swaab, 409–31. Edinburgh: Elsevier.

Li, Weicon, Jer-Ming Chen, John Robert Smith, and Joe Wolfe. 2015. "Effect of Vocal Tract Resonances on the Sound Spectrum of the Saxophone." *Acta Acustica united with Acustica* 101: 270–78. DOI: 10.3813/AAA.918825.

Manning, Erin. 2016. "For a Pragmatics of the Useless, or the Value of the Infrathin." *Political Theory* 45, no. 1: 1–19. DOI: 10.1177/0090591715625877.

Minh-ha, Trinh T. 1986/7. "She, the Inappropriate/d Other." *Discourse* 8: 3–10.

Naylor, Paul. 1999. *Poetic Investigations: Singing the Holes in History.* Evanston: Northwestern University Press.

Nwadike, Chinedu. 2000. "Tidalectics: Excavating History in Kamau Brathwaite's *The Arrivants.*" *IAFOR Journal of Arts and Humanities* 7, no. 1: 55–67. DOI: 10.13140/RG.2.2.20826.80325.

Reckin, Anna. 2003. "Tidalectic Lectures: Kamau Brathwaite's Prose/Poetry as Sound-Space." *Anthurium: A Caribbean Studies Journal* 1, no. 1: 1–16. DOI: 10.33596/anth.4.

Rutherford-Johnson, Tim. 2010. "Rambler Roundtables: ELISION Ensemble." *The Rambler*, February 1. https://johnsonsrambler.wordpress.com/2010/02/01/rambler-roundtables-elision-ensemble/.

Ryan, David, and Helmut Lachenmann. 1999. "Composer in Interview: Helmut Lachenmann." *Tempo* 210: 20–24. DOI: 10.1017/S0040298200007154.

SenseLab. "Anarchive—Concise Definition." *Senselab — 3e*. https://senselab.ca/wp2/immediations/anarchiving/anarchive-concise-definition/.

Siegel, Ethan. 2017. "A 200 Year Old Lesson: Scientific Predictions Are Worthless Unless Tested." *Medium,* March 17. https://medium.com/starts-with-a-bang/a-200-year-old-lesson-scientific-predictions-are-worthless-unless-tested-6f88797d267b.

Singh, Julietta. *No Archive Will Restore You*. Earth: punctum books, 2018.

Sterne, Jonathan. 2003. *The Audible Past: Cultural Origins of Sound Reproduction*. Durham: Duke University Press.

Toksöz Fairbairn, Kevin. 2016. *ay neden şeftali gibi kokuyor?* Self-published.

Tsing, Anna Löwenhaupt. 2015. *The Mushroom at the End of the World: On the Possibility of Life in Capitalist Ruins*. Princeton: Princeton University Press.

Tschumi, Bernard. 1996. *Architecture and Disjunction*. Cambridge: MIT Press.

Voegelin, Salomé. 2010. *Listening to Noise and Silence: Towards a Philosophy of Sound Art*. New York: Continuum.

Volcler, Juliette. 2013. *Extremely Loud: Sound as a Weapon*. Translated by Carol Volk. New York: The New Press.

Zornberg, Avivah Gottlieb. 2009. *The Murmuring Deep: Reflections on the Biblical Unconscious*. New York City: Schocken Books.

www.ingramcontent.com/pod-product-compliance
Lightning Source LLC
Chambersburg PA
CBHW051131160426
43195CB00014B/2424